the
kickboxing
handbook

the
kickboxing
handbook

John Ritschel

Published by SILVERDALE BOOKS

An imprint of Bookmart Ltd

Registered number 2372865

Trading as Bookmart Ltd

Blaby Road

Wigston

Leicester

LE18 4SE

© 2004 D&S Books Ltd

D&S Books Ltd

Kerswell,

Parkham Ash, Bideford,

Devon, England,

EX39 5PR

e-mail us at:

enquiries@dsbooks.fsnet.co.uk

This edition printed 2004

ISBN 1-845090-38-1

DS0127 Kickboxing Handbook

Creative director: Sarah King

Project editor: Clare Haworth-Maden

Photographer: Colin Bowling

Designer: Axis Design Editions

Fonts: Helvetica, Eurostile

Printed in China

1 3 5 7 9 10 8 6 4 2

contents

introduction

You may think that writing an introduction to kickboxing would be a straightforward task, and that explaining what it is and what it stands for would be easy. There are many ways to view this martial art, however, for martial artists practise kickboxing as a sport, an art or a lifestyle.

Kickboxing has been around for over thirty years and has a strong international following. It incorporates kicking and punching and requires flexibility, body alignment, confidence, speed and endurance. Above all, it teaches you how to defend yourself.

This is a sport that can reduce body fat, help you to develop a lean body and is very good for reducing stress. Practising kickboxing for only two hours a week on a regular basis can result in a life-enhancing body awareness. It is one of the best ways in which to exercise: you will burn off excess fat, relieve stress, enjoy yourself and make lots of great friends.

This kind of exercise beats going to the gym, with its lonely and boring workouts. When practising martial arts, you will interact more with people than you would ever do in a gym. Another great feature of kickboxing is that you will learn discipline, self-confidence, respect for your opponent and how to overcome your limits.

This book is designed to guide you through various aspects of the sport and to motivate you to reach and overcome the targets that you set yourself. It explains the history and background of kickboxing and the different aspects of this explosive martial art. It introduces you to the equipment and skills that you will need to get started and defines the training schedules for the grades and eventually sparring or fighting in the ring. Different techniques for stances, kicks, punches, jumps, sweeps and blocks are discussed, too, as well as how to combine them into advanced techniques.

This book also looks at the techniques needed to upgrade to a black belt. It will give you the necessary knowledge to design your personal kickboxing strategy to meet your needs and to decide which techniques work best for you. That's why the main emphasis is on a step-by-step guide to mastering certain aspects of the techniques. First, though, the importance of warming up and stretching is underlined before any training, sparring or even competition fighting is addressed.

Above all, this book underlines how rewarding kickboxing can be, and how it can make you a more balanced person.

Kickboxing incorporates all of the elements of an effective martial art, and can lead to increased fitness and reduced stress, as well as body fat.

1: the development of kickboxing

In order to understand the roots of kickboxing, one has to understand the principles of martial arts. Martial arts are systems, or traditions, of unarmed and armed combat, whose aim is often to develop the character and skill of the practitioner.

Due to their overexposure through films, television programmes and magazine articles, the martial arts are popularly believed to be of eastern Asian origin. Yet it would be incorrect to say that martial arts are unique to Asia. Different cultures have always had to defend themselves against attackers, with or without weapons. It is this tradition of defending yourself against an attacker that helps to define a martial art. Systems of fighting have always developed alongside strategies of conflict. The history of martial arts is thus both long and borderless.

The gladiators of ancient Rome and knights of Europe trained in martial arts in order to survive. We can therefore classify archery, fencing, wrestling and boxing as Western martial arts. But these ancient arts are not as popular as the martial arts that we know today.

The core of a martial art is a standardisation of practices and traditions which, when practised over and over again, results in mastership of the system. This mindful application of techniques and force is a characteristic of a good martial artist.

Martial arts are often classified as 'hard' or 'soft' styles, with hard styles being classified in turn as 'external' and soft styles as 'internal'. The external style is a powerful, high-speed martial art, whereas the internal style places more emphasis on rounder and softer movements.

The following are some examples of a few soft, or internal, styles.

Aikido is classified as a non-violent martial art that uses mainly locks and throws. It uses an opponent's force against him or her by means of rapid movements and counterholds. Because of these restraining, non-violent features, aikido is used by the Japanese police to control suspects.

Hsing-i chuan, also known as chinese mind-boxing, is based on the five elements:wood, water,

Aikido: a soft, or internal, martial art.

Tai chi is another soft,
or internal, martial art.

earth, metal and fire, which represent five basic movements: splitting, crushing, pounding, drilling and crossing.

Tai chi chuan is an art that is frequently practised in slow motion. The training emphasis lies in the connection of one's chi (energy) with the earth. The practice of tai chi improves balance, co-ordination, concentration, circulation and overall health.

Wing chun is said to be a soft style of kung fu that uses effective techniques from other kung-fu styles. Wing chun uses no high kicks, instead concentrating on low-level kicks and hand and finger strikes with which to defeat an attacker. The most famous martial artist to have his roots in wing chun was Bruce Lee.

The following are some examples of hard, or external, styles.

Karate, which means 'empty hand', has its roots in the Japanese island of Okinawa. Because using weapons was against the law on Okinawa, the islanders had to learn to defend themselves empty-handed. Karate includes hard kicks, punches and blocks that are practised by means of sparring and forms.

Tae kwon do is a Korean martial art, and one of the most popular in the world. It is characterised by rapid, high kicks and energetic body punches. It is believed that tae kwon do has the largest arsenal of kicks of any martial art.

Although 'kung fu' is the term used for all Chinese martial-arts' styles, some of the well-known external styles are lau gar and hung gar. Each style places different emphases on kicks and hand techniques. The most famous kung-fu forms are probably the animal techniques.

Unsurprisingly, Thai boxing originated in Thailand. It is a very practical martial art whose main philosophies are simplicity and effectiveness. The chief difference between Thai boxing and other martial arts is that it uses strikes with the elbows and knees. In the early days of Thai boxing, hemp gloves dipped in a mixture of ground glass and glue were used to generate terrifying-looking injuries.

So into what category does kickboxing fall? Is it an external, or hard, or internal, or soft, style? Looking at the external styles, it is clear that kickboxing is also an external, or hard, style. Kickboxing has its roots in such traditional martial arts as Thai boxing, tae kwon do, karate and kung fu. It even uses judo techniques to sweep an opponent off-balance. Kickboxing is sometimes referred to as a 'ring sport', which it indeed is, but looking at its roots, it becomes clear that kickboxing is a very effective martial art, too, one that takes just as long to master and perform gracefully as any traditional martial art.

Kung fu is a hard, or external, martial-arts' style.

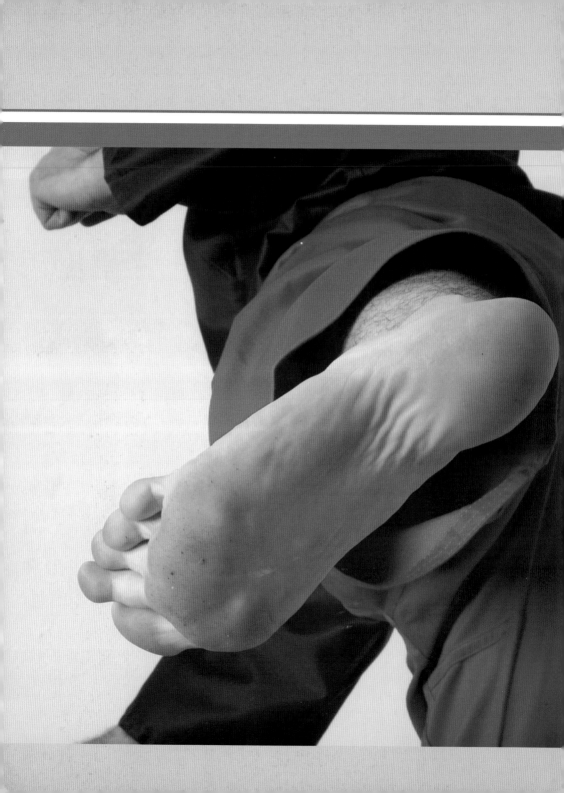

2: the history of kickboxing

Kickboxing is a relatively modern martial art that combines boxing techniques with kicks. A combat sport, kickboxing has its roots in traditional martial arts, including as it does techniques from karate, Thai boxing, tae kwon do and kung fu.

Martial arts gained in popularity during the early 1970s, and karate practitioners in America soon became frustrated with the strict controls and rules entrenched in set rituals that did not allow full-contact kicks and punches and fights to the knockout. They wanted to see how effective their fighting style was in a realistic situation.

And so it was that kickboxing originated in the United States, where traditional martial arts took on a more Westernised style, and where those of their practitioners who wanted to concentrate on tournament fighting were inspired to develop kickboxing.

Kickboxing is different from traditional combat sports like Thai boxing in that it prohibits strikes with the elbows and knees. All of the techniques practised in this combat sport are directed above the belt.

Because of the great emphasis that was placed on specialised punching and kicking techniques being used at maximum force against an opponent, questions were raised about safety and the high risk of injury in this new sport. As a result, protective clothing like groin guards, gum shields and hand and foot pads designed to lessen the impact of the kicks and punches, as well as improved safety rules, were introduced. The most notable was the introduction of weight divisions ranging from flyweight to super heavyweight (see page 18).

Such martial artists as Bill 'Superfoot' Wallis, Demetrius Havanas, Jeff Smith, Mike Warren, Joe Lewis, Blinky and his brother, Benny, were among the first generation of kickboxers involved in staging very successful events. All of these fighters were the best of the best in this new martial art. The first full-contact world championships were held in Los Angeles in September 1974, the legendary Bill Wallis, Joe Lewis, Jeff Smith and Isuena Duenas becoming the first full-contact world champions.

It was martial artists like Howard Hansen (a black belt in karate who was one of the main promoters of kickboxing) who first staged fights in a boxing ring instead of the usual karate tournament bouts. Hansen later became known as 'The Ring Matchmaker'.

It was in those early days that the World Kickboxing Association (WKA) was founded. The WKA became successful by finding common ground between Western and Eastern full-contact fighting culture, thereby creating and defining a culture for the sport that improved the recognition of full-contact competitions.

Today, kickboxing is a sport that is practised not just by hard-core, full-contact fighters, but also by people who want to develop strength, flexibility, stamina, fitness and well-being. These aspects of kickboxing appeal to both men and woman, whatever their background. It is not a brutal sport in which people meet in backyards and beat the hell out of each other. It is a powerful and skilful sport that improves mental agility and fitness and also promotes comradeship. Kickboxing is practised by celebrities, too, including film stars like Jean Claude van Damme, a Belgian actor whose nickname is 'The Muscles From Brussels'.

different kickboxing styles

There are a lot of different styles of kickboxing. Every style has its own rules, which can differ from organisation to organisation.

Fights are normally supervised by a body affiliated to a particular organisation. The length of a fight can range from three to twelve rounds, each round being two minutes long. The rest time between the rounds is usually one minute. After each round, points are awarded. Once the final bell has been rung, the fighter with the most points is declared the winner, which is known as winning by decision. The fight can also be won by a knockout blow if a full-contact style is being fought.

Because of the nature of the sport, kicks have to be used in a fight. The general rule is that you have to place at least eight kicks per round. The points system used during fights is normally as follows: a punch =1 point; a kick to the head = 2 points; a kick to the body = 1 point; a jumping kick to the body = 2 points; a jumping kick to the head = 3 points.

In kickboxing, fights are usually divided into weight divisions. Refer to page 18 for a table showing the different weight divisions specified by the World Kickboxing Association.

semi-contact

In semi-contact kickboxing, points are awarded for punches and kicks that are delivered with reasonable force. After every successful strike, the fight is stopped and points are awarded. The length of the fight is normally two rounds, each round lasting two minutes. The compulsory safety equipment is kick boots, gloves, a groin guard, a mouth guard, a shin guard and a head guard.

weight divisions: men

Flyweight	Up to 50.5kg (111lb)
Super flyweight	Over 50.5 and up to 52kg (115lb)
Bantamweight	Over 52 and up to 53.5kg (118lb)
Super bantamweight	Over 53.5 and up to 55.5kg (122lb)
Featherweight	Over 55.5 and up to 57kg (126lb)
Super featherweight	Over 57 and up to 59kg (130lb)
Lightweight	Over 59 and up to 61kg (134lb)
Super lightweight	Over 61 and up to 63.5kg (140lb)
Welterweight	Over 63.5 and up to 67kg (148lb)
Super welterweight	Over 67 and up to 70kg (154lb)
Middleweight	Over 70 and up to 72.5kg (160lb)
Super middleweight	Over 72.5 and up to 76kg (168lb)
Light heavyweight	Over 76 and up to 79kg (174lb)
Super light heavyweight	Over 79 and up to 83kg (183lb)
Cruiserweight	Over 83 and up to 86kg (190lb)
Super cruiserweight	Over 86 and up to 90kg (198lb)
Heavyweight	Over 90 and up to 95kg (209lb)
Super heavyweight	Over 95kg (209lb)

weight divisions: women

Women's weight divisions range from 48kg (106lb) to over 64kg (141lb),

with the weight class changing every 2kg (4lb).

light contact

Light contact is an intermediate stage between the semi-contact and full-contact styles. Light contact uses controlled techniques. The fight is continuous and is not stopped after every strike as it is with semi-contact. The only time that the fight is stopped is when clinching occurs. The length of the fight is normally two rounds, each lasting two minutes, with a one-minute rest between rounds. The compulsory safety equipment is kick boots, gloves, a mouth guard, a groin guard, a shin guard and a head guard.

full contact

Full-contact kickboxing bouts are fought in a ring. As the name suggests, full-contact fighters are allowed to throw kicks and punches at maximum power. Knockouts can therefore be seen in full-contact fights. Amateur bouts consist of three rounds, with one-minute breaks between rounds, each round lasting two minutes. The length of each fight can vary, however. Professional bouts can last for twelve rounds. The compulsory safety equipment is

kick boots, gloves, a groin guard, a mouth guard, a shin guard and a head guard (but those in professional bouts will not wear head guards).

thai boxing

Thai boxing is a full-contact sport. It is different from full-contact kickboxing, however, in that low kicks and knee and elbow strikes can be directed to the body and head. (But note that although elbow strikes are allowed in professional bouts, they are not permitted in amateur bouts.) Amateur bouts last for three rounds, with each round lasting three minutes. Professional bouts last for five rounds, with each round lasting for three minutes. The compulsory safety equipment is gloves and a gum shield. No protective gear may be worn on the legs and feet. Amateur fighters will also wear head guards, whereas professionals will not.

3: is kickboxing for me?

Due to modern training techniques, kickboxing has become the ultimate workout. It produces kickboxers who are strong, fast, fit and very conditioned. Kickboxing training gets you into top physical shape, toning your body by reducing body fat.

Kickboxing offers an intense cardiovascular workout. That it also teaches the art of self-defence is very appealing to a lot of people. It is therefore not surprising that taking kickboxing classes has become one of the biggest trends in the fitness industry since aerobics.

women in kickboxing

Kickboxing appeals to the young and old, to men and woman. Indeed, it is becoming increasingly popular with women as a practical means of learning to defend themselves while also becoming fit; it promotes a positive mental attitude, too. Women find the training aspects of kickboxing attractive because they can help to burn fat and quickly tone and firm the body. A lot of women today compete internationally at the highest levels of kickboxing.

Kickboxing is additionally a practical martial art that does not seem as monotonous as many traditional martial arts. The basics can be learned in about six months.

age in kickboxing

Age does not matter in kickboxing. What does matter is that practitioners know what they want from the training. Children can start as early as ten, and it is important that parents chose a good club in which all beginner's classes are strictly no contact, progressing to controlled sparring with no contact to the head. Sparring must be closely supervised, and fully protective clothing and a head guard must be worn.

The upper age limit is a question of mental attitude. There are martial-arts' practitioners in their sixties performing workouts that some twenty-year-olds would find hard to follow. Martial arts prompt a positive mental attitude that makes barriers vanish. Remember that we set our own barriers, and that age should not be one of them.

is kickboxing a dangerous sport?

Some people think of kickboxing as being an extreme sport that is rife with injuries. This perception could not be further from the truth, and some kickboxers would assert that playing football or rugby can be a lot more injurious than kickboxing. It is important to understand that in the advanced stages, both training and sparring are closely supervised and consist of more than just lashing out at each other.

Communication is another important factor in training safely. Talk to your training partner to make it clear to what level you want to take it. Tell your partner either that you want to take it easy or that you want to spar seriously.

When competition fights are fought, the fight is monitored so closely that hardly any major injuries occur.

how long does it take to learn kickboxing?

The basics of kickboxing can be learned in approximately six months or so, during which time you can participate in all of the normal training routines. Mastering kicks and punches and using them in fighting strategies against different opponents can take years, however.

Sometimes, the less you think about performing techniques, the more naturally they come. This will occur the more experience you gain in kickboxing. Good kickboxers always look loose and not tense, which is one of the reasons why their reactions are faster and they do not use up as much energy as beginners.

So to answer the original question: it takes years to become a technically competent kickboxer.

do you have to be fit to practise kickboxing?

As is the case with any sport, it helps to be fit to practise kickboxing, but if you are not, you should still be fine as long as you are physically healthy and don't have any serious health problems. A good club should point out that you can only do your best, and that the only person who can really push you is you yourself.

After just three months of training twice a week, you will notice the difference: you will feel fitter and will be starting to look leaner. The time when fitness is paramount is when you wish to compete because the fitter you are, the easier you will find it to survive the rounds. If you are not fit and are struggling to keep going, this is when your techniques will become slack and less powerful. To achieve fighting fitness, it is probably fair to say that you should train at least five times a week.

where do I find a good club?

The best place in which to look for a good kick-boxing club is your local library, which should have an index of clubs in your area. Visit your local clubs to get a feel for them. When selecting a club, it is vital to ask yourself whether you could see yourself working with the people that train there because they will get the best out of you. A good club should have a friendly atmosphere, take pride in its safety measures and emphasise good techniques. Remember that a club should serve to teach you how to become a better fighter, not to inflict injuries on you.

what sort of equipment do I need?

It is important to remember that you should always train with high-quality equipment, and that the equipment that you hit, or hit with, is durable.

clothing

Kickboxing trousers usually have an 8cm (3in), boxer-style, elasticated waistband. They are generously cut to enable a lot of movement and allowance is also made for a groin guard.

The top is usually a club T-shirt or jacket; the belt indicates the grade attained.

safety equipment

You will firstly need boxing gloves. Their weight may be 227 or 286g (8 or 10oz) for men, depending on the competition, but are always 286g (10oz) for women. Secondly, you will need padded footwear, and thirdly, a head guard, so that both your opponent and you are protected. Fourthly, boxing bandages will protect your hands and will give you a firm hold when you are wearing boxing gloves. The fifth, optional, requirement is shin guards, which will provide protection from impact when you are sparring or competing.

The mouth guard is a very important safety device that should be worn at all times when you are sparring and, of course, when you are competing in the ring. It is important to opt for a good-quality mouth guard. As a rough guide, the better and tighter the mouth guard fits, the more protection you will have. Note that you could buy a mouth guard that protects both your upper and lower jaw (when wearing it, you should clamp your teeth together and breathe through the integral breathing hole).

As its name suggests, a groin guard will protect your groin against any impact, particularly when high kicks are being performed, the groin being a target that can be unintentionally hit. The groin guard is a hard-plastic guard that has an elastic strip for a secure fit. It is worn under kickboxing trousers.

hand-wrapping

It is crucial to wrap your hands with boxing bandages because this will support your fingers and wrists, thus reducing the risk of injury. It also provides extra padding within your boxing gloves. When wrapping bandages around your hands, always start with your left hand and finish with your right hand.

There are different ways of wrapping your hands. Experiment to find the most comfortable for you.

wrapping your hand

1 Place your thumb in the bandage's loop.

2 Then wrap one-third of your forearm before working back towards your wrist.

3 Circle your thumb a couple of times.

4 Start circling your knuckles.

5 Now begin securing the bandage through your fingers. The result should resemble the picture at left.

grading in kickboxing

Kickboxing has a similar grading system to that of any other martial art. However, the grading syllabus differs from organisation to organisation. There are usually eight belts before the black belt. Grading begins with the white belt, which indicates a novice. It then continues with the red, yellow, orange, green, blue, purple, brown, and finally, black belt, which it can take between three to four years to attain.

The grading syllabus normally consists of elements of fitness, kicks, punches, hand techniques, defence techniques, shadow sparring and sparring.

grade	
	white belt
	red belt
	yellow belt
	orange belt
	green belt
	blue belt
	purple belt
	brown belt
	black belt

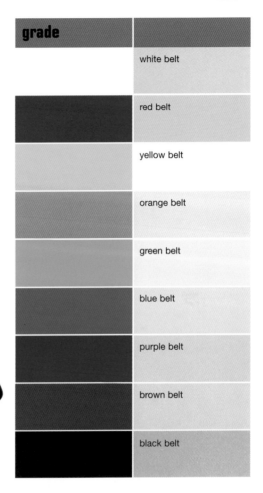

Examples of grading syllabus

The grading syllabus outlined below is typical for the yellow belt, but can, of course, vary from organisation to organisation.

fitness

Two minutes skipping;
twenty press-ups;
twenty abdominal crunches;
twenty squat thrusts.

kicks

Five front kicks;
five roundhouse kicks;
five axe kicks.

punches

Five jabs;
five crosses;
five jab and crosses.

grading for a black belt

A typical grading syllabus for a black belt is outlined on these pages. As you will see, a person's physical fitness and fighting ability have to be very good in order to achieve a black belt.

fitness

Eight minutes skipping;

sixty press-ups;

sixty abdominal crunches;

sixty squat thrusts.

kicks

(All of the kicks have to be performed for both sides.)

Five front kicks;

five side kicks;

five roundhouse kicks;

five axe kicks;

five turning back kicks;

five heel kicks;

five turning heel kicks;

five double roundhouse kicks with a step;

five heel kicks and roundhouse kicks with a step;

five double side kicks with a step;

five jumping front kicks;

five jumping roundhouse kicks;

five jumping, turning roundhouse kicks;

five jumping, turning back kicks;

five jumping, turning heel kicks.

punches and hand techniques

Five jabs;

five crosses;

five cross and hooks;

five jab, cross and jabs;

five jab and uppercuts
   performed with the same hand;

five double jab and crosses;

five jab, cross and hooks;

five retreating jabs;

five jab, slip and uppercuts;

five slip, hook and crosses;

five jab, cross, roll and hooks with the same hand;

five retreating jab and uppercuts;

five retreating jab and hooks with the same hand;

five retreating jab, uppercut and hooks with the
   same hand

five retreating jab, uppercut and hooks with the
   same hand and place a cross.

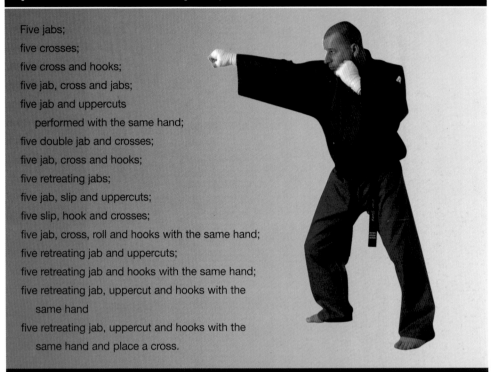

defence techniques

Sparring against given attacks.

sparring

Shadow sparring;

sparring.

Grading in kickboxing has many advantages. It focuses your mind on the requirements needed to pass the next grading, for example. When training for your next belt, you will also practise your moves over and over again, helping to ensure that your techniques become second nature, and that you reach the stage at which you don't have to think about them, you just perform them. A further advantage is that your physical fitness will improve with each grading.

4: warm-up exercises

Warm-up exercises serve to prepare the muscles for exercise, also increasing the blood flow to them. To prevent injuries, it is important to warm up the whole body thoroughly before undertaking any exercise.

The warm-up exercises should gently stretch and loosen your main muscle groups in preparation for the more intense stretching exercises that follow.

Warm-up exercises should never involve any sudden movements. The movements should feel comfortable. If they don't, you should stop and analyse what you are doing wrong, or even consider the possibility that you may have an injury. If you feel uncomfortable at any stage, stop the exercise.

When warming up, work your way from the top of your body to the bottom.

The whole warm-up routine should not take longer than ten to fifteen minutes.

neck warm-up

Repeat the exercises below ten to fifteen times.

1 Stand with your feet a shoulder-width apart. Relax, and move your chin gently forward, towards your chest.

2 Now bring your head back up and relax the stretch.

3 Look straight ahead and tilt the left side of your face towards your left shoulder.

4 Now release the tension and tilt your head to the right.

5 Turn your head so that you are looking left.

6 Release your stance and turn to the right.

shoulders warm-up

Hold the stretches below for up to thirty seconds.

1 Stand with your feet a shoulder-width apart. Tilt your head to the left while pulling down your right hand with your left hand.

2 Now reverse the movement so that your head is tilted to the right and you are pulling down your left hand with your right hand.

3 Bring your right arm across your chest and hold it in a stretch with your left arm.

4 Now bring your left arm across your chest and support it with your right arm.

5 Begin to move your arms in small circles.

6 Then move your arms in increasingly large circles until they are turning in the largest-possible circles.

arms warm-up 1

The following warm-up exercises concentrate on the biceps and
triceps. Warm-up exercises 1 and 2 will warm up your biceps,
while warm-up exercise 3 will work your triceps.

1 Raise your arm to shoulder height and place
the back of your hand against a stationary
object so that your thumb is pointing at
the floor.

2 Rotate your body away from your hand; this
works your biceps.

Perform the exercise for about thirty
seconds with each arm.

arms warm-up 2

You work your biceps when performing this exercise. It is important to perform the movement fifteen to twenty times in a smooth and continuous manner. Do not use force.

1 Stand up straight and point the palms of your hands behind you.

2 Now try to lift your arms towards the ceiling behind your body. While you are doing this, twist your palms outwards.

arms warm-up 3

For this exercise, try to position the palm of your hand between your shoulder blades until you feel a stretch. Keeping your chin up, gently push back your elbow with your other hand. Hold the stretch for about thirty seconds and then switch sides.

chest warm-up 1

The following warm-up exercises will effectively warm up your chest. In order to avoid injury, they should be performed in a controlled and slowly flowing manner.

1 Raise your arm to shoulder height and place the palm of your hand against a stationary object so that your thumb is pointing at the ceiling.

2 Rotate your body away from your hand; this works your chest.

Perform the exercise for about thirty seconds with each arm.

chest warm-up 2

1 Place your finger-tips behind your ears. Raise your elbows to shoulder height and look straight ahead.

2 Now pull back your elbows until you feel a stretch. Repeat the exercise twenty times.

chest warm-up 3

1 Stand with your feet a shoulder-width apart. Cross your arms in front of your body, relax and look straight ahead.

2 Pull back your arms and twist your palms so that they are pointing at the ceiling. It is important to perform this movement smoothly. Do not use too much force.

Perform this exercise twenty times.

back warm-up 1

Because back injuries can easily occur, it is important to try to avoid them by controlling the back exercises.

1 Stand with your feet a shoulder-width apart. Then clasp your hands together and, with your elbows bent, push your arms forward. Your chin should be pointing at your chest. Push your arms forward until you feel a stretch in the middle of your back.

2 Release both the tension and your hands and bring your elbows back again.

This exercise should be performed ten to fifteen times.

back warm-up 2

1 Get down on your hands and knees. Tuck your chin into your chest and curve your spine.

2 Now relax, straighten your back and release your chin from your chest.

Perform this exercise ten times.

back warm-up 3

This warms up the sides and lower back.

1 Stand with your feet a little more than a shoulder-width apart and keep your knees slightly bent.

2 Now switch sides. Make sure that your supporting hand is on your hip and that your other hand is above your head when you lean to the side.

hips warm-up 1

In kickboxing, the leg and upper-body movements are very much dependent on good hip flexibility. It is therefore important to warm up the hips properly.

1 Stand with your feet a shoulder-width apart, with your hands on your hips.

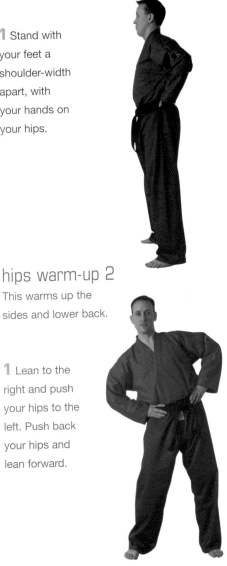

2 Lean back and push your hips forward.

hips warm-up 2

This warms up the sides and lower back.

1 Lean to the right and push your hips to the left. Push back your hips and lean forward.

2 Lean to the left and push your hips to the right. Now rotate your hips, ensuring that your eyes remain focused in front of you.

legs warm-up 1

Repeat this exercise ten to fifteen times.

1 Stand with your feet a shoulder-width apart and put your hands on your hips.

2 Now slowly bend your knees, keeping your body upright and your back straight. Slowly descend until your legs form a 90-degree angle.

When ascending to return to the starting position, make sure that your knees are slightly bent.

legs warm-up 2

1 Stand with
your feet
together and
place your
hands on
your knees.

2 Then push your
knees forward.

legs warm-up 3

1 Holding your
right foot, pull your
heel towards your
bottom. Try to hold
this position for
twenty to thirty
seconds.

2 Now do the
same with your
left leg.

If necessary, rest
your hand against a
wall in order to
keep your balance.

5: stretching for improved kicking

On the following pages, we concentrate on stretches that will improve your kicking. In order to be a good kicker, it is important that your legs, groin and hips are flexible.

Flexibility also depends on your hip, knee and ankle joints moving freely. It is therefore important to work on the flexibility of your hamstrings, upper thighs, the backs of your legs and your calf muscles. By doing this, you will also work on your joints and improve their freedom of movement. The stretches described here progress from beginner to expert level.

When you are working on the flexibility of your lower body, it's essential to understand that you are working on the strongest, and most powerful muscles, in your body. This is why you should ensure that you only stretch to a point of tension where you still feel relaxed. Do not push too hard because this will be counterproductive. It is important to concentrate on stretching continuously and steadily. Your body will tell you when to stop, so listen to it.

When you stretch regularly, you will improve your flexibility. The only thing that you have to remember is that it takes time and dedication.

Having completed the warm-up session outlined in the previous chapter, concentrate on developing flexibility for your kicks by performing the exercises on the following pages.

sumo squat

The sumo squat is an excellent exercise for stretching the adductors in your inner thighs.

Position your feet wide apart, making sure that they are pointing outwards. Now press your forearms against your inner thighs and lower yourself into a squatting position until you feel a little tension. Remain in this position for twenty to thirty seconds.

Perform this exercise about three times.

knee bend

The knee bend is designed to stretch the quadriceps, the muscles in the front of the thighs. Standing on your right leg, hold your left foot with your left hand. To intensify the stretch, pull the heel of your foot towards your bottom and push your hips forward. Hold the stretch for about thirty seconds.

Switch sides and stretch the quadriceps in your right thigh.

front-lunge position

In the front-lunge position, you are stretching the hip flexors in the mid-section of your upper thighs. Stand upright, with your feet a shoulder-width apart, and then go into the front-lunge position. Place your hands behind your back for support, and to keep your back straight. Remain in this position for twenty to thirty seconds.

one-leg hip hinge

The one-leg hip-hinge position is designed to stretch your hamstrings. Move one foot forward and straighten your leg, keeping your back leg slightly bent. Now lean forward, place your hands on your bent leg and pivot your body; you should feel a stretch in your straight leg. Hold this position for twenty to thirty seconds.

forward bend

The forward bend is a very good stretch for the lower back, the trunk extensors and the ham-strings. Stand with your feet together and bend forward. To support the stretch, grab your ankles and pull your chest gently towards your legs. If you cannot reach your ankles, use your calf muscles to lower yourself. Hold this position for ten to thirty seconds.

angular leg extension

The angular leg extension is a very important exercise for improving your kicking flexibility. As well as working your hamstrings, it stretches your inner thighs and lower back.

Sit on the floor and spread your legs as wide as possible, ensuring that your feet are pointing upwards. Reach for and hold your foot, and then pull your body towards it. Stay in this position for ten seconds before switching sides.

Perform this exercise three or four times for each side.

static dancer

The static dancer is an exercise that will stretch the gluteals and piriformis in your bottom. Position your front leg in a 'V" shape in front of your body and straighten your back leg. With your elbows in front of you to support you, lower your upper body towards your chest. Hold the stretch for about thirty seconds. Raise your upper body and stretch again before changing sides.

pretzel

The pretzel will work your outer and inner thighs and lower back. This exercise will give you a very good stretch in preparation for the kicks that you will perform. When you kick, you will twist your body and stress the afore-mentioned muscle groups, which is why it is important to prepare them by stretching them.

Position your left leg in a 'V' shape in front of your body and then place your right leg over it. Ensure that your upper body is perfectly straight. Now place your left elbow against your right leg and apply pressure to the knee. Position your right arm behind your back to support your upper body. Remain in this position for ten to thirty seconds before switching sides.

pancake stretch

The pancake stretch will stretch your inner-thigh muscles (the adductors). This stretch is very safe, and not as radical as the splits.

Sit on the floor with your knees bent and the soles of your feet touching one another. Position your hands around your ankles and then try to push your knees towards the floor. If you are able to do so, then try to push your chest towards your feet; this will intensify the stretch. Hold this position for five to ten seconds, then release the tension and repeat five to ten times.

side-kick stretch

The side-kick stretch will work your inner thighs. This stretch works best when a partner pushes your leg so that you can gradually put more tension into the stretch.

First assume a normal side-kick position by turning your hip and pointing your foot downwards. Your partner should position his or her foot against your static foot to prevent you from slipping before placing your ankle on his or her shoulder and then slowly and gradually applying tension until you say 'stop'.

Because kickboxing is a sport that trains almost every muscle in your body, it is important to develop your strength in order to perform its techniques in a controlled manner.

As you improve your aerobic fitness, you should introduce elements of strength-training to your exercise programme. Strength-training involves performing activities that require short bursts of power and muscular strength.

Good muscular strength has a positive effect on your appearance because it improves your muscle tone and shape, as well as your posture. It also helps to avert lower-back problems and stabilises your joints. Muscular strength is vital in preventing injuries because the muscles support fragile joints and improve balance. All of these afore-mentioned points are important for an athletic or healthy lifestyle.

The following exercises, which use your own body weight, are safe and easy to perform in a training hall or gym.

strengthening the legs

Repeat this exercise up to twenty-five times.

1 Stand in front of a step, with your feet a shoulder-width apart. Now position your right foot on the step.

2 Now position your left foot next to your right foot

3 Jump off the step and start the exercise again.

strengthening the calf muscles

Repeat this exercise up to twenty times

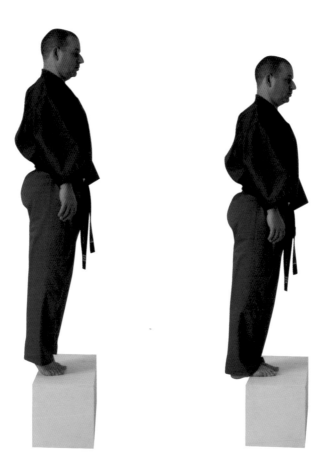

1 Stand on tiptoe on a step, ensuring that your heels do not come into contact with it. Using your calf muscles, push your body upwards and then hold this position for four seconds.

2 Lower your body and hold this position for another four seconds.

strengthening the hamstrings and buttocks

Repeat this exercise up to twenty times for each side.

1 Supporting your body with one knee, place both of your hands on the floor. The leg that you are about to exercise should be raised, with your foot pointing at the floor.

2 Pull your foot towards you until your leg is bent at a right angle and then straighten it again.

strengthening the hamstrings and buttocks

Repeat this exercise ten times for each leg.

1 Assume a standing position and then chamber your leg as though you were placing a kick.

2 Now straighten your leg and hold this position for two seconds before bringing your leg back down again.

strengthening the outer thighs

Repeat this exercise fifteen times for each leg.

1 Resting on your forearm and hip, lie on your side, with your bottom leg bent.

2 Raise your straight leg, but make sure that you do not lift it more than 45 degrees.

strengthening the back muscles

Repeat this exercise three times.

1 Lie on your stomach and stretch
out your arms and legs.

2 Now lift your arms and legs off the
ground and hold this position for up
to twenty seconds.

strengthening the stomach muscles 1

1 Lying flat on your back, bring up your knees to an angle of about 90 degrees.

2 Using your stomach muscles, slowly lift your upper body. It is important to keep your back rounded, but do not arch your back.

strengthening the stomach muscles 2

1 Lie on the floor, with your arms by your sides. Now bend your knees so that your calves are at a 90-degree angle to the floor.

2 Using your stomach muscles, push your legs away from you. Hold this position for about four seconds and then slowly lower your legs back down to the floor.

strengthening the shoulders, arms and chest

Perform the press-ups up to fifty times, depending on your level of fitness.

1 Assume the press-up position, with your hands slightly more than a shoulder-width apart. It is important to keep your back straight.

2 Now lower your body until your groin is about 2.5cm (1in) above the floor and then push it up again.

strengthening the triceps

Repeat this exercise twenty to thirty times.

1 With your legs held straight out in front of you, support yourself by placing your hands on a chair or step behind you.

2 Now lower yourself until your arms are bent at an angle of a little more than 90 degrees and then straighten them again.

strengthening the sides

Repeat this exercise ten to fifteen times on one side. Then perform it ten to fifteen times on the other side.

strengthening the bottom

Repeat this exercise twenty to thirty times.

Position your feet a shoulder-width apart. Keeping your back straight, lower your body and then rise up again.

1 Lying on your side, position your elbow on the floor and then raise your body.

2 Now lift your leg, hold this position for two seconds and lower your body to the floor again.

strengthening the legs and shoulders

Clench your fist at least fifty times.

1 Assume a low horse-riding stance, then raise your arms in front of you and clench your fists ten times.

2 Now hold out your arms to the sides and clench your fists ten times. Return to the starting position.

cardiovascular training

Cardiovascular, or aerobic, training enhances the heart and lungs' ability to deliver oxygen to the muscles while exercising. If it is to pump more blood around your circulation system, it is therefore important to develop the strength of your heart. This will enhance both your aerobic and anaerobic capacity.

Typical cardiovascular exercises include running, walking, swimming, rowing, cycling and even climbing stairs. These exercises will make your heart beat faster and provide a constant flow of blood to the active muscles. Having an increased heart rate will improve the performance of the cardiac muscles, in turn enhancing your endurance.

If you want to become fitter, it is probably fair to say that your fitness will be improved more by the intensity of the exercise than by either its duration or frequency. High-intensity exercise will therefore increase your endurance.

Swimming regularly is good for an all-round excerse regime

running

Running (also called roadwork) is an important factor in a kickboxer's training schedule because it is an easy way in which to enhance fitness. There are different methods of running, however, with interval runs, anaerobic-interval runs, hill runs and speed-play runs being the most beneficial for kickboxers.

running is an excellent form of cardio-vascular exercise.

interval runs

Interval runs are hard runs that require 100 per cent effort and last for two to eight minutes. You should then allow yourself an equal amount of recovery time. This type of run will benefit you greatly by increasing to the maximum the amount of oxygen that your muscles can consume.

anaerobic-interval runs

Anaerobic-interval runs are very hard sprints lasting from thirty seconds to two minutes, with a recovery time that is twice as long. The benefit of this type of run is increased speed through the utilisation of fast-twitch muscle fibres.

hill runs

Hill runs involve running up a hill and then down again at a slower pace. The basic principle is, the steeper the hill, the tougher the workout. The major benefit of this exercise is that your leg muscles will gain in strength.

speed-play runs

Speed-play runs are runs that combine many of the afore-mentioned types of run in one workout. The benefit of this is that your body becomes used to different paces

No matter how skilled you are as a kickboxer, your training will include working with various pieces of equipment, such as focus mitts, focus paddles, Thai pads and kicking shields.

focus mitts

By using focus mitts, you will develop speed, power and timing, and will learn to aim at a specific target. When the mitts are moved into different positions, you will learn to react quickly and to adapt to a target. Above all, they will give you an excellent workout. With focus mitts, you can chose to place a punch or kick, and because they force you to focus on a very small striking area, they will increase your accuracy. The most important lesson to be learned is that of judging distance, in that you will begin to develop an instinctive feel for the distance to a target. You will also learn how to adjust your stance in order to place an effective kick or punch. Almost all kickboxing combinations can be practised with focus mitts.

exercise 1

1 Place a left jab.

2 Follow up with a right cross.

3 Now direct a roundhouse kick at the head.

4 Then turn the focus mitt and place a turning hook kick.

exercise 2

Focus mitts can be used for avoiding punches and counter-attacking. These exercises will develop your defensive skills, will help you to practise your boxing and kicking combinations and will teach you to throw kicks and punches from a variety of angles.

1 The person wearing the focus mitts should throw a hook towards the puncher and should then bob and weave out of reach of the returning hook.

2 The puncher should now approach and direct a hook at the focus mitts.

3 The focus mitts should now be held at midsection height before a roundhouse kick is placed.

4 The focus mitts are now raised so that a roundhouse kick can be placed at head height.

the focus paddle

The focus paddle is an excellent training tool for improving your kicks. Its advantage is that as the target, it is somewhat removed from the body of the person holding it. You can therefore practise kicks that you would not normally attempt in case you hit him or her.

Other advantages are that you follow through and totally concentrate on your technique, and not on the power of the kick.

1 The first technique that can be practised with a focus paddle is a spinning hook kick.

2 Now try a spinning crescent kick.

exercise 1

3 Now try a roundhouse kick.

4 Without dropping the roundhouse kick, bring back your leg with a hook kick.

exercise 2

1 With a focus paddle, you can also practise jumping kicks. Try a front jumping kick.

2 Practise your jumping crescent kick, too.

thai pads

Because Thai pads are very well padded, they take the impact of a blow extremely effectively, giving the person holding them extra protection. They are also light, which means that they don't restrict your mobility. The versatility of Thai pads is demonstrated below and on the following pages.

1 In order to avoid injuring the person holding them, aim at the middle of the Thai pads.

2 Direct a roundhouse kick at the middle of the Thai pads.

3 Practise your knee strikes on Thai pads.

4 Work on your elbow strikes.

place-punching combinations

A back fist can be placed with the maximum power because the person holding the Thai pad is holding it away from his or her body.

A hook can similarly be placed with the maximum power.

kicking shield

When training, the kicking shield is a very useful piece of equipment for practising kicks. Because it is large, it gives the person holding it extra security. The kicks that are directed at a kicking shield include all kinds of side kicks, front kicks and roundhouse kicks.

1 Direct a side kick at the middle of the kicking shield.

2 The size of the kicking shield lessens the risk of injury to the person holding it.

3 Direct a front kick at the middle of the kicking shield.

4 Now try to deliver a spinning back kick to the middle of the kicking shield.

distance training with focus mitts, a kicking shield and thai pads

Timing and distance are very important for kickboxers.
This exercise is a perfect way of improving both.

exercise 1

1 Your partner, wearing focus mitts, starts to walk towards you. Shuffle backwards and direct a jab at the focus mitts.

2 Continue to walk backwards and place a right cross on the focus mitts.

3 With your opponent walking away from you, repeat steps 1 and 2. You will have to adjust your stance in order to reach him or her.

4 Continuing to walk forwards, direct a right cross at the focus mitts.

exercise 2

1 In order to improve your kicks and learn more about distance and timing, move backwards and forwards in front of a kicking shield.

2 Now hop back and execute a side kick.

3 The side kick slams into the middle of the kicking shield.

exercise 3

1 Because the person holding the Thai pads is moving away, his opponent has to perform a small jump when executing a roundhouse kick in order to hit them.

2 Now the person holding the Thai pads is simulating an attack by moving towards the kicker, making the scenario seem more realistic.

3 The kicker gains space by jumping backwards before performing a roundhouse kick.

4 The roundhouse kick hits the Thai pads.

8: stances and footwork

It is vital to understand the importance of a stance and how to move out of it. Mastering this movement and preparing for the next kicking or boxing technique is crucial for any good fighter.

The stance is the foundation of all attacks and defences, and the more flowing your techniques, the faster you will be able to react and defend yourself, attack or counterattack.

It is vital to understand that all kicks and punches should be executed in a normal boxing stance. This stance allows you to perform any kick or punch, although you will probably have to make slight adjustments to your stance at times in order to deliver certain kicks.It is used in order to move into any technique without making your intentions obvious.

It is important to be light on your feet and to feel comfortable in your fighting stance. The famous phrase that the boxer Mohammed Ali used was: 'Float like a butterfly and sting like a bee'. When you watch footage of Ali, you soon realise how important footwork is. See the stance as the beginning of any technique in kick-boxing. And the faster your footwork, the faster you will be in executing your techniques.

Because this squared-off position is so versatile, the fighting stance (see page 92) allows you maximum freedom of movement. It gives you a relatively low centre of gravity, enabling you to move from one side to another, as well as backwards and forwards.

fighting stance

The fighting stances for the right- and left-handed fighter are shown below. The following explanation is for a right-handed fighter, but if you are left-handed, simply substitute 'left' for 'right' and so on.

Stand with your feet a shoulder-width apart, with your left foot about 60cm (2ft) in front of your right foot and both feet pointing slightly to the right. (Having your feet pointing to the right means that your body is turned to the side and presents your opponent with a reduced target area.) Ensure that your knees are slightly bent and keep your fists at chin level, with your lead hand a little extended. (This will enable you to protect your midsection at the same time as protecting your head with your fists.) Sixty per cent of your weight is on your front leg, but this can be adjusted, depending on the technique.

Fighting stance for the right-handed fighter.

Fighting stance for the left-handed fighter.

t-stance

When you compare the fighting stance with the T-stance that is used in more traditional martial arts, it becomes apparent that the weight distribution is different. In the T-stance, seventy per cent of your body weight is placed on your back leg, for example. It is an excellent stance if you are a good kicker and your kicking leg is in front of your body. However, this stance makes it hard to place a right cross without distributing your weight, and when you are distributing your weight, you are signalling to your opponent that you are about to place a punch. It is therefore important to learn to place any technique in the kickboxing fighting stance.

The T-stance is an effective stance, but be warned that it limits your movements.

The traditional T-stance.

The T-stance seen from the side.

mobility

In kickboxing, good mobility and footwork are just as important as being able to kick and punch. Fighters who don't work on their footwork can look jerky and tense. The faster you are on your feet, the more graceful and quicker you will become. When your stance and footwork are good, you will also make better use of your body, in turn resulting in more powerful techniques.

Your ability to move from one position to another must become second nature because when you fight, you move either back and forth

or from side to side at speed. Your balance and stability depend on you being able to maintain a good stance and sound footwork when you are moving quickly. If your stance is unstable, you will not have a good foundation on which to perform kickboxing movements and techniques. Not only will they lack power, but it will be hard for you to balance your body correctly if your stance is not right and your footwork lacks co-ordination. Able footwork and a good stance distinguish a good kickboxer from a less able one.

footwork

The photograph on page 94 shows two kick-boxers working on their footwork in an exercise that is essential for partners. When one partner is said to lead, this means that he or she goes forwards, backwards and sideways, with the other following. Not only are they practising their footwork, but working on their reactions and getting a feel for distance. Advanced kickboxers train in this way very quickly indeed.

Footwork is an extremely important factor when learning essential fighting techniques. Good footwork is vital if you are to attack and defend effectively because it determines your distance from your opponent. Footwork is always a starting point for any technique, for kicks and punches alike.

Footwork has to be mastered in order to ensure that you keep your balance in every possible situation. In order to achieve this, you have to practise it regularly so that every move becomes second nature. Even very experienced fighters practise their footwork over and over again, for every powerful punch or kick originates in good footwork.

Good footwork, coupled with a good stance, enables you to manoeuvre yourself into any position ready to kick, punch or block. Your opponent is not stationary, which means that you will have to learn to manage your space in order to be ready to take advantage of any opportunity. If your footwork is competent, you should be able to judge the correct distance to enable you accurately to place any technique that you wish to perform.

footwork when moving forwards

Your footwork will be displayed when you come out of a fighting stance. If you move forwards, you will move your leading leg first, and will drag your rear leg after it shortly afterwards. This move is called a 'step-drag'. When performing a step-drag, remember never to cross one foot over the other because this will prevent you from tripping over your feet.

1 The footwork is performed when coming out of a fighting stance

2 Move your front leg and position it in front of your body.

3 After you have positioned your front leg, drag your rear leg into position.

footwork when moving backwards

If you move backwards when coming out of a fighting stance, you will move your rear leg first and will drag your front leg after it shortly afterwards. This move is called a 'backwards step-drag'. When performing a backwards step-drag, do not cross your legs because you will lose your balance if you do so.

1 The footwork is performed when coming out of a fighting stance.

2 Move your back leg and position it behind your body.

3 After you have positioned your back leg, drag your front leg into position.

footwork when moving to the side

If you move sideways when coming out of a fighting stance, you will first move the leg that is closest to the side to which you want to move, and will then drag the leg that is further away towards it. When you perform this 'side-step drag', do not cross your legs because this would put you off-balance.

moving to the left

1 The footwork is performed when coming out of a fighting stance.

2 Move your left leg and position it to the left of your body.

3 After you have positioned your left leg, drag your right leg to the left, into position.

Follow steps 2 and 3, substituting 'right' for left' and 'left' for 'right', when moving to the right.

pivoting

Pivoting is important because it enables you to achieve maximum results using minimal movements. As a defensive application, it can both get you out of a difficult position and create an opening for a counterattack. Pivoting can also be used as an offensive application to enable you to move into a better attacking position. It can be performed clockwise or anticlockwise.

1 Start in a fighting stance, with your right foot and lead hand in front of your body. Your weight should be on your front leg; move your back leg as shown here.

2 Pivot through 90 degrees, either staying in a fighting stance or moving into a counter-attacking stance.

moving forwards

If the step-drag movement does not enable you to cover the required distance and your opponent is out of reach, you will have to use a movement that will quickly allow you to gain ground without changing your lead hand. The movement demonstrated below and opposite will enable you to do so.

1 Start in a fighting stance. If your left hand is your lead hand, push your left foot forwards. If your right hand is your lead hand, substitute 'right' for 'left' and 'left' for 'right' when reading these instructions.

2 Move your left foot and step forwards 10cm (4in) in order to keep your balance. If you don't perform this step, the momentum will have to be provided by your rear leg, which will slow you down.

3 Now position your rear leg behind, and parallel to, your front leg.

4 Step forward with your left foot. You may be surprised how much ground you can cover when you've mastered this technique.

moving backwards

If a backwards step-drag cannot take you the required distance, you will have to use a movement that will enable you to cover that extra ground. So follow the steps illustrated on pages 102–3, but moving in the opposite direction.

When performing both the forwards and backwards movements, it is important to understand that your feet should be merely millimetres (not even an inch) above the floor throughout the whole exercise.

1 stepping with a lead-hand change

The footwork for this movement may look natural, but in order to perform it well, as well as to be ready for any situation, it is important to be light-footed. This very aggressive, forward-moving motion can be used to change your lead hand or to gain momentum before throwing a rear-leg kick.

1 Start in a fighting stance. Begin to transfer your weight to your front leg.

2 When all of your weight is on your front leg, change your lead hand to your right hand. Your rear leg is now free to move forwards, so that your right foot and right hand are in front of your body.

2 jumping step

The jumping step offers a very quick way of gaining space. When you use the jumping step instead of the normal forward step, you will cover a distance of 2.5m (about 8ft) in just three-quarters of a second rather than one-and-a-half seconds. This movement is therefore ideal whenever you need to gain space quickly in order to attack or retreat.

3 forward-jumping step

1 Start in a fighting stance.

2 Gain upward momentum by whipping your arms up. As you transfer all of your weight on to your front leg, your rear leg should start moving forwards. Pushing off on your front leg will launch you forwards.

3 After you have landed on the ground, it is up to you whether you kick or punch. The side kick is being executed here.

To perform a backwards-jumping step, reverse the instructions given here.

stances in combination with footwork

It is crucial that you appreciate the importance of a good stance in combination with good footwork. The same basic principles apply when performing all of the applications outlined in this chapter: relax your upper body, be light on your feet, turn your hips and shoulders with the step, don't stagger (in order to keep your balance) and always keep your guard up. The more you practise your footwork, the better and more light-footed you will become.

Also remember that you should not only use the movements in this chapter to move forwards, backwards, to the left and to the right, but should practise modifying them in order to move diagonally. The diagonal motion combines all of the principles mentioned above.

By modifying the footwork that you have learned, you will begin to control your space better and more efficiently. By moving diagonally, you will also be able to move in and out of an attacker's range. If you only move in a straight line, you will create an easier target for your opponent, which is the last thing that you want to do, and why it's important to work on your diagonal footwork.

9: punches

Before we discuss boxing techniques, it is important to look at the basics and to stress the fact that repetition is the key to mastering a technique and then performing it to the best of your ability.

Even when you are an experienced fighter, you will find that continuing to work on the basics proves how important repetition is, for if you repeat a technique often enough, it will become second nature. It may be a long journey, but repetition will make you a good martial artist.

Until you master the basics, you will feel uncomfortable performing the more complex moves, and this will show in your technique. For instance, combinations will look rigid when you perform them, and a sequence will appear as though it consists of three or four movements put together rather than one, flowing movement.

Another point that it is important to accept is that boxing techniques are crucial in kickboxing. It often seems as though fighters who are good kickers feel that they can neglect their boxing techniques. The message is simple, however: be good at both kicking and boxing techniques, and you will be able to use more fighting strategies against different fighters. When you watch fights, you will soon realise that excellent kickers always use their kicking techniques to dominate a fight. Yet if you also have good boxing techniques, you can step into the kicker's range, work your punches and frustrate your opponent's fighting strategy.

This is the correct way to position your hand to avoid injury when punching.

1 Bend your fingers to form a fist.

2 Then position your thumb under the knuckles of the first two fingers.

3 The striking area. To avoid injuring yourself, always try to punch in such a way that the largest two knuckles connect with your target.

the jab

The jab is probably the most basic punch that you can learn in boxing. It is also the most important. It is not the most powerful, however, and should be practised in combination with other kicks and punches.

The jab can be used to keep an opponent away from you or to set you up to perform a follow-on technique. It can be used to test opponents, too, enabling you to see how they react, how they block and how fast they are. It can also be used to mislead and distract an opponent before you execute your own technique.

The jab can be used to deliver punches to the head or body, be it as a single punch or in rapid succession. You can use it to defend yourself from attack or as an attacking technique.

It is therefore important to learn how to throw a jab while you are moving backwards, forwards and sideways. Jab techniques can be used with a step in order to throw your bodyweight behind the punch, but they can also be performed from a stationary position when an opponent is within your reach or stepping into your space.

1 Start in a fighting stance, with both hands raised to protect your body. Your lead, or right, hand should be in front of your body and your left hand should be protecting your face.

2 When you jab, turn your fist so that your palm is facing downwards. This will add a whip-like effect to your movement. Remember to turn your body into the punch.

3 When you place the punch and your fist is fully turned, it is important to think about defence. It should therefore be as though your left hand is glued to your face, while your jaw is protected by your shoulder (tuck your chin behind your shoulder).

4 Pull back your fist and assume a fighting stance, with your fists and arms protecting your face and body.

the right cross

The right cross, which is also referred to as the 'straight right', is a very powerful punch that can achieve a lot of knockouts. Like the jab, it can be directed at the head or body.

The right cross can be used as an attacking, defending or counterattacking technique. It is very powerful as a counterattacking technique because when opponents attack you, they bring their body weight forward, so that when you punch, the combination of your opponent's body weight and your own will help you to land a very powerful punch, to devastating effect.

When executing this punch, it is important to throw your body weight into it, which means that you will have to pivot on your rear leg in order to obtain a better reach and add power to your punch.

1 Begin in a fighting stance, with your lead hand in front of your body and your right hand at the side of your face.

2 Turn your fist so that your palm is facing downwards. Turn your body into the punch

3 As you fully extend your arm and place the punch, make sure that your chin is tucked behind your shoulder to protect it from any blows. Pivot on your rear leg in order to put your body weight behind the punch. Snap back your fist and assume a fighting stance.

the hook

The hook is a very effective technique that results in more knockouts than any other punch. This is because you throw your body weight behind it. It can be directed at the head or body, depending on the situation in which you find yourself and the targets that are open to you.

Rather than moving straight forward, when executing the hook, your body makes a rotating twist on its own axis in order to generate power. Your front leg pivots on its foot, bringing your body weight forward, and you should also rotate your shoulder and hip. It is important to throw your whole body weight into the hook and then to follow through in order to give your punch speed and power.

1 Assume a fighting stance.

2 Turn your fist so that your palm is facing downwards.

3 When executing the hook, your body should make a rotating twist and your arm should be moving in an arc parallel to the ground. Pivot on your front foot and throw your body weight behind the punch. Then snap back your fist and assume a fighting stance, with your guard up in order to protect your body and face.

the uppercut

When you watch kickboxing fights, it becomes apparent that many fighters neglect the uppercut. When performed well, however, it can be a nasty punch that can result in a knockout. It is only when some fighters are at the receiving end of an uppercut that they realise that it is a very effective weapon to include in their fighting arsenal.

The uppercut can be classified as a close-range punch that travels directly upwards to connect with an opponent's chin, floating ribs or solar plexus.

The uppercut's power is generated by turning the shoulders and hips and by bending the knees and then straightening them before impact. If this sequence is performed seamlessly, the punch will have a tremendous impact. Although it can be executed with your lead (left) or right hand, a right-hand uppercut will always generate more power than a lead- or left-hand uppercut.

1 Assume a fighting stance.

2 Turn your fist so that your palm is facing towards you. Turn slightly to the right and bend your knees.

3 Now generate maximum power by straightening your knees and turning your shoulders and hips to produce an upward surge with your whole body. Then snap back your fist and return to the fighting stance. Due to the nature of the punch, you remain very near to your opponent and may consequently now wish to use other kicking or punching combinations.

the back-fist strike

The back-fist strike is a fast strike that can be used to distract or disorientate an opponent. It is not a very powerful punch, but it can set you up to use any kicking or punching combination, such as a kick or a powerful right.

When executing a back-fist strike, aim at the side of the head, which you should hit with your knuckles.

1 Assume a fighting stance, with your lead hand in front of your body and your right hand by the side of your face.

2 Pull back your lead hand and body before striking. Your lead hand should move across your face.

3 Place your back-fist strike so that your knuckles connect with the side of your opponent's head. Remember to follow through with your whole body.

You could follow this strike with a boxing combination, but if you don't, make sure that you raise your guard when resuming a fighting stance.

the spinning back-fist strike

The spinning back-fist strike can be remarkably effective as a surprise attack. This punch is a fast strike that can be used in combination with any other strike or kick.

It is important to appreciate that the power of this punch is generated by spinning the body, the head and torso being turned in order to see the target. As you come around in the spin, you should cock your arm at the elbow, and to generate a whipping motion, you should strike the target as you come around and not before, or after, you have completed the spin.

The striking area for the spinning back-fist strike is the side of the head, which you should hit with your knuckles.

1 Start in a fighting stance; your lead hand and front leg should be your left hand and left leg.

2 Pivoting on your left foot and cocking your striking arm at the elbow, spin through 180 degrees clockwise, making sure that you turn your head as fast as possible.

3 Remember that the motion of turning generates this strike's whipping power. Hit the target after you have completed the spin.

4 The striking area is the side of the head.

After executing the strike, resume a fighting stance.

the overhand right

The overhand right is a mixture of a right cross and a hook, but with its own characteristics.

The right cross remains aligned with your head, whereas the hook is punched in a path that is slightly curved. The overhand right follows a curved path above an opponent's head.

The overhand right can be an effective way to get past an opponent's defences, and its targets are the temple, jaw or ear. In order to get around the opponent's guard and find the perfect angle for this punch, it is important to execute a short step to the side.

1 Start in a fighting stance; your lead hand and front leg should be your left hand and left leg.

2 Take a short step to the left and bring your right hand over your opponent's head.

3 As you place the punch and fully extend your arm, make sure that your fist's two main knuckles connect with the target. Pivot on your rear leg to throw your weight behind the punch.

Snap back your fist and assume a fighting stance or follow on with boxing combinations.

As its name suggests, kickboxing includes a variety of kicks. These are similar to the kicks that are performed in other martial arts, but tend to be those that are the most effective in the ring.

Before we discuss any kicks, it is important that you are familiar with the foot's various striking areas. These are: the ball of the foot (1); the top of the foot (2); the sole of the foot (3); the foot's inside edge (4); the foot's outside edge (5); the bottom of the heel (6); and the back of the heel (7). (See also the following pages.)

Remember that it is important to position your toes and foot properly, as well as to use the correct striking area, if you are to execute a good kick and minimise the risk of injurying yourself.

striking areas

Below you can see the correct position of the foot and toes and the striking areas are highlighted through the lighter area on the foot.

1 The toes are pulled back before the ball of foot is used.

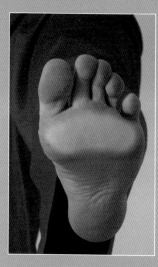

2 The toes are pointed before the top of the foot is used.

3 The foot is flexed backwards before the sole is used.

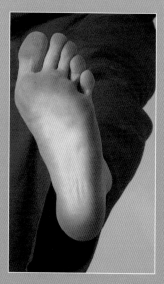

4 The toes can either be
pulled back or pointed before
the foot's inside edge is used.

5 The toes can either be pulled
back or pointed before the foot's
outside edge is used.

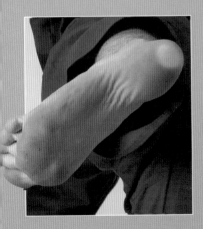

6 Pull back the toes
before using the bottom of
the heel.

7 Pull back the toes before using the
back of the heel.

Kickboxing uses kicks as its bread-and-butter techniques because of the power and range that they give a fighter.

Kicks are therefore seen as being an important part of a kickboxer's success, and intensively practising their movements, speed and power will always result in both graceful and explosive techniques.

Although kicks are the hardest element of this martial art to learn and master, doing so is not only most satisfying, but makes the difference between a good and a very good kickboxer.

It is important to understand that the whole body is involved in a kick, not just the leg and foot. To make the kick more effective, your body can move either towards or away from the target, depending on the kick that you are performing. It is the motion of your body that gives you an extra surge of power.

Another crucial point to appreciate is that your hips should turn with the kick, thereby maximising its power because you are injecting the force of your body weight into the technique. Using your hips will give you greater reach, too, because you hold your body far looser, enabling you to reach higher when kicking.

It is also vital to understand the importance of positioning your foot correctly when placing a kick. In order to obtain the best position for most of the kicks, you should direct the heel of the pivoting foot on the ground at the target. (This is less commonly done for a front kick, however.)

Once you have mastered the kicking techniques outlined in this chapter, they will be among your most powerful tools. If your kicks are powerful and fast, and you have good control over them, your opponent will have difficulty influencing the fight. Kicks can be executed just as quickly as punches, but from further away, and the feet are also more resilient than the hands. You can generate three times as much power with a kick then you can with a punch, but this power can only be released when the correct techniques are used. (More energy is required to perform a kick than a punch, however, while athletes with long legs will have a major advantage over opponents with shorter legs.)

These are just some of the reasons why kickboxers spend so much time focusing on improving their kicks. Kicking is also an excellent cardiovascular workout. In addition, learning defensive and offensive kicking techniques, as well as the necessary footwork and body movements, requires you to use all of the major muscle groups simultaneously.

Every time that a kick is performed, the front and side abdominal, or stomach, muscles are used to raise the leg in readiness for that kick. Kicking will therefore tone and strengthen your abdominal muscles in particular, thereby protecting you from injuries and helping you to endure kicks and blows to your body. Having strong abdominal muscles will allow you to twist your body more, too. And because the abdominal muscles connect your upper body to your lower body, if they are strong, they will help you to produce a more dynamic kick.

If you are to perform them well, and to merge them effectively later, it is vital that you understand the differences between the various kicks, as outlined on the following pages.

the front kick

The front kick is the first to be learned in most martial arts because it is simple and fast. When performed well, it can be used in tournament fighting and sparring. You can perform it with your front or back foot as an advancing or stopping technique. It can be a snap or push kick.

the front snap kick

To perform a front snap kick, raise your kicking leg in front of you and chamber it towards your target, so that you raise and bend your knee. The striking area for this kick is the ball of the foot, which is why you should pull back your toes and aim your foot at your target before snapping it

1 Assume a fighting stance, with your fists raised to protect your body and head.

2 Raise and bend your knee into the chamber position. Ensure that your foot is pointing at your target.

3 Pull back your toes. Pivot on your supporting leg to enable your other hip to whip round and the ball of your foot to make contact with your target.

out towards him or her.

To make it more powerful , it is important to remember to lean towards your target when performing the front snap kick.

This kick can also be executed with the front leg, in which case you would have to move back onto your rear, supporting leg and push yourself forwards with it.

4 Snap back your foot into the chamber position and pivot back around on your supporting leg.

5 Position your kicking leg either in front of your body or behind it, in the starting position, whichever you prefer.

the front push kick

The front push kick can be seen as an offensive or defensive kick, depending on how it is executed. When the front leg is raised and pushed towards the opponent, it can be used a defence. When a strike is made with the sole of the foot, it can be used to fend off attackers. This technique is very useful because it enables you to give your opponent a big push, thereby throwing him or her off-balance after blocking an attack. This push can provide you with sufficient distance in which to attack or counterattack by aiming follow-up

1 Assume a fighting stance, with your fists raised to protect your body and head.

2 Pull your attacking leg up, towards your chest, ensuring that your knee is fully bent, your toes are pulled back and your foot is flexed.

3 Kick out with the sole of your flexed foot. When placing the kick, lean into it and pivot on your supporting leg to enable you to use your hip.

kicks at your opponent. (These follow-up tactics and counterattacks will be discussed when we look at combinations and follow-up techniques.)

The front push kick can be performed with the front or rear leg. It is important that you lean forward into the kick and raise your knee as high as possible before placing the kick.

The striking area is the sole of the foot. In order to avoid injuring yourself, pull back your toes and flex your foot before kicking out.

To make it more powerful , it is important to remember to lean towards your target when performing the front push kick.

This kick can also be executed with the front leg, in which case you would have to move back onto your rear, supporting leg and push yourself forwards with it.

4 Snap your foot back into the starting position and pivot back on your supporting leg.

5 Position your kicking leg either in front of your body or behind it, whichever you prefer.

the roundhouse kick

The roundhouse kick is probably the most frequently used kick in sparring and competition fighting. When you watch competition fighting, it becomes apparent that the roundhouse kick is used on average four times as often as any other. It is therefore a very important kick to master.

Often used to attack or counterattack, this kick is very versatile and can easily be used in combination with other kicks and hand techniques. It is a very fast and powerful kick that can deliver a powerful blow to the side of an opponent's head or body.

It is important to lean into the roundhouse kick in order to move forwards. This kick can

1 Assume a fighting stance, with your fists raised to protect your body and head.

2 Point your toes, bend your knee and push your kicking leg back, towards your target.

3 Keep your toes pointing at your target before the top of your foot connects with it.

also be used defensively, when you will move backwards (this technique will be explained later, in connection with sparring).

The striking area is the top of the foot, which should be pointed at the target to facilitate its placement at the side of the head or body.

Before placing the kick, your lower leg should be moving parallel to the ground. When placing the kick, lean into it and pivot on your supporting leg. The heel of your supporting foot should be pointing at the target before turning your foot 180 degrees.

4 Snap your foot back into the starting position.

5 Position your kicking leg either in front of your body or behind it, whichever you prefer.

the side kick

The side kick is renowned for its graceful appearance and powerful impact. It is one of the hardest basic kicks to learn, but is a very useful technique to have in your competition arsenal.

The side kick can be executed with the front or back leg and serves as an attacking or defensive technique. Fighters with long legs tend to rely on it as a front-leg technique to be used as a defensive technique against an attacker.

The front-leg side kick does not differ greatly from the rear-leg side kick; it is just a question of where to balance your body weight. Which kick

1 Assume a fighting stance, with your fists raised to protect your body and head.

2 Bend your knee as you pull your kicking leg towards your chest, with your heel pointing at your target. It is important to chamber your leg as high as possible and to pivot on your supporting leg through 180 degrees so that your heel is pointing at the target.

you use will be determined by the distance between you and your opponent, and this will be discussed in the sparring section.

To perform the perfect side kick, it is important to align your ankle, knee, hip and shoulder in a straight line, and not to let your shoulder move out of alignment.

The striking areas are the heel or outside edge of the foot. In order to avoid injuring yourself, pull back your toes and flex your foot.

This very useful technique can be quick and effective when used in a variety of combinations, which will be discussed later.

3 When placing the kick, remember to direct your foot's striking area at the target. Your foot and leg should not dip or curve, but should travel in a straight line. Your foot should be flexed on impact, and your toes should be pointing downwards so that you can twist your hip into the target.

4 Position your kicking foot either in front of your body or behind it as you assume a fighting stance again.

the axe kick

The axe kick is executed by raising the sole of your foot above your opponent's head, and when it reaches its highest point, pulling it down towards the target. A useful technique, the axe kick is easy to learn.

As well as the sole of the foot, the axe kick can be performed with the ball, or even the heel, of the foot. The version of the axe kick that uses the heel is the most powerful strike, and when your kicking leg is raised, you will feel the tension in the back of it. Using the sole or ball of the foot will give greater height, however. Remember to pull back your toes and flex your foot in order to protect yourself from injury.

1 Assume a fighting stance, with your fists raised to protect your body and head.

2 Keeping your knee straight, raise your kicking leg as high as you can before forcefully pulling it down. It is at this stage that you should pivot on your supporting foot and turn your hip into the kick.

You can use your supporting leg's forward motion to move towards your opponent before striking. But be careful when performing the axe kick, especially when you are inexperienced, because the momentum and force of the kick can knock you off your supporting leg, causing you to fall over.

The axe kick can be performed with either the rear leg or front leg (use the front leg for a quick attacking or counterattacking kick). It can be executed with a straight or bent knee, and it is important to use both options for different situations when training.

When you have practised it often enough, you can use the momentum generated by this kick to slide forwards and cover the distance between you and your opponent.

3 Keeping your knee straight, pull down your leg as hard as you can. The maximum power is concentrated at head height.

When you bring your leg back down, do not stamp your foot on the ground. Control the impact by leaning forwards after placing the kick.

4 Position your kicking leg in front of your body in a fighting stance that is the opposite of the one that you assumed in step 1.

the crescent kick

The crescent kick is very closely related to the axe kick. However, the difference between the two is that when you are performing the crescent kick, the inside or outside of your foot will sweep across your body in a clockwise or anticlockwise arc rather than travelling in a straight line, as would occur for the axe kick.

There are two types of crescent kick: the outside crescent kick and the inside crescent kick. As their names suggest, in the first, the circular motion is started from the outside, and in the second, it is started from the inside.

Before executing a kick, you have the choice of performing either a straight-leg kick or a bent-knee kick for a faster release. With the crescent kick, you also have the option of using your front

or rear leg, although kickboxers are more likely to use the front leg to perform a strike in a fighting situation.

The striking area can be the heel or outside or inside of the foot. Make sure that your toes are pulled back and that your foot is flexed.

Prepare to execute either crescent kick by assuming a fighting stance, with your fists raised to protect your body and head.

the outside crescent kick

The outside crescent kick describes a circular motion, with the straight leg moving from the inside to the outside of the body.

1 With all of your body weight on your supporting leg and your hands forming closed fists, straighten your rear leg and pull it forwards.

2 Swing your leg across your body, and when it reaches its highest point, strike the side of your opponent's head with the outside of your foot.

3 After making the strike, let your leg continue to travel in an arc to the outside of your body. Remember that it is important to lean into the kick in order to control your balance.

4 At this point, you have the option of releasing your leg into a bent chamber or continuing the straight-leg kick. Another choice is between moving forwards and positioning your foot in front of your body or positioning it to your rear.

the inside crescent kick

The inside crescent kick describes a circular motion, with the straight leg moving from the outside to the inside of the body.

1 With all of your body weight on your supporting leg and your hands forming closed fists, straighten your rear leg and pull it forwards.

2 Swing your leg across your body, and when it reaches its highest point, strike the side of your opponent's head with the inside of your foot.

3 After making the strike, let your leg continue to travel in an arc to the inside of your body. Remember that it is important to lean into the kick in order to control your balance.

4 At this point, you have the option of releasing your leg into a bent chamber or continuing the straight-leg kick. Another choice is between positioning your foot in front of your body or positioning it to your rear.

the outside spinning crescent kick

The principle behind the outside spinning crescent kick is similar to that behind the inside crescent kick, except that the kicking leg is lifted from behind the turning body. This helps you to gain ground when moving towards an opponent. With practice, this kick can be performed extremely quickly.

This technique can be used as an attacking or counterattacking kick that can inflict a powerful blow on an opponent. When performing this kick, you will be turning your back on your opponent, which is why it is important to turn your head towards your target as quickly as you can to ensure that you do not lose control of the situation.

You could perform this kick with a bent or straight leg, depending on the distance between you and your opponent.

This kick is typically performed to mislead an opponent, who will be expecting a back or hook kick, but not an outside spinning crescent kick.

1 Assume a fighting stance, with your fists raised to protect your body and head, as well as to aid your balance. Turn your head and the heel of your front, supporting leg towards your target and then place all of your weight on your supporting leg.

2 Your shoulder, head and supporting foot should all be directed towards your target before you move your kicking leg, otherwise your hip will get in the way of the kick.

3 It is essential to pivot on your supporting foot when performing this kick. Pull up your kicking leg as though you were performing a normal outside crescent kick.

4 When your leg reaches its highest point, either strike the side of your opponent's head with the outside of your foot or let it crash down into a guard position.

5 At this point, you have the option of releasing your leg into a bent chamber or continuing the straight-leg kick.

the back kick

The back kick is a favourite weapon in many a kickboxer's arsenal because of the power that it can generate. As well as being powerful (and it is not uncommon to see it delivering a knockout blow to the body), it can be performed very quickly. This kick is so powerful partly because the gluteus maximus, the largest muscle in the body, is used to execute it and partly because of the energy that is produced when turning into it.

The back kick can be used as an attacking or counterattacking technique. When it is used as a retreating technique and the kicker is moving backwards, it still unleashes great power. And when the fighter is counterattacking, the back kick does not offer an opponent any targets, which is why it is valued as a safe kick.

The striking area is the heel. Before executing this kick, pull back your toes and flex your foot in order to avoid injurying yourself.

1 Assume a fighting stance, with your fists raised to protect your body and head. In order to place a back kick, it is important to turn your supporting foot through 180 degrees towards your target. Your head should be turning on the same side as your kicking leg and your shoulder should be pointing towards your opponent. Never lose sight of your target.

2 With your weight on your supporting leg, move your kicking leg forward from the rear. The back kick is different to the side kick in that the knee is not lifted, but instead stays low and close to the supporting leg.

3 Execute the back kick by kicking your kicking leg straight behind your supporting leg. Your foot should travel from the ground to your target.

Depending on the situation, you should then place your foot either in front of you or, if you are retreating, behind you.

the hook kick

The hook kick can be regarded as the opposite of the roundhouse kick because it uses the heel or sole as the striking area rather than the top or ball of the foot. It may take time to master, but when this kick is performed perfectly, it is fast, very powerful and can result in a knockout.

The hook kick can be executed from either behind or in front of the body, but is probably faster when performed from in front of the body. When it is performed from behind the body, it can catch an opponent out, however, because he or she may be expecting a roundhouse kick.

1 Assume a fighting stance, with your fists raised to protect your body and head.

2 Chamber your kicking leg as high as possible. This position is exactly the same as for the side kick (see page 136, step 2), and it is similarly important to pivot your supporting heel through 180 degrees so that it is pointing towards your target.

But the attacker moves past the opponent's body and then attacks again with the hook kick.

This kick is mainly used to strike an opponent's head. If it is to succeed, it is therefore very important to have hip flexibility.

The striking area is the heel or sole of the foot. Remember to pull back your toes and to flex your foot in order to avoid injury.

3 With your leg travelling from the side, aim the kick at your opponent's head. Your leg should be straight when your heel or sole connects with the target.

4 Snap your leg past your opponent and chamber your leg again as you continue to turn back into the starting position.

5 Position your leg in front of your body and resume the starting position.

the spinning hook kick

The spinning hook kick is often used as a defensive kick. Because it requires excellent balance and very flexible hips, it is a hard kick to master, however. The difference between this kick and the normal hook kick is that the spinning hook kick incorporates a turn of 360 degrees, so that it looks like the beginning of a normal back kick (see pages 148 to 149) to start with. But instead of executing a back kick, it is a hook kick that you perform.

1 Assume a fighting stance, with your fists raised to protect your body and head.

2 In order to place a spinning hook kick, it is important to turn your supporting foot through 180 degrees towards your target. Your head should be turning on the same side as your kicking leg, your shoulder should be pointing towards your opponent and you should be looking over the same shoulder.

It is vital to pivot on your supporting foot in order to follow the kick through. Just go along with the momentum because if you resist it, the kick will not look controlled and you will be thrown off-balance. It's also important to lean into the kick so that you don't fall backwards when placing it, so push your weight forwards and execute a push with your supporting leg.

The striking area is the heel or sole of the foot. Remember to pull back your toes and to flex your foot in order to avoid injury.

3 Make sure that your weight is on your supporting leg when your kicking leg moves from the rear. This kick differs from the normal hook kick in that the knee is not lifted, but stays low and close to your supporting leg. Direct your kicking leg straight behind your supporting leg. Your foot should travel in an arc from the ground to the target. Your leg should be straight, and your foot should be flexed and your toes pointing downwards on impact.

4 By the time that you position your foot to the rear of your body in a fighting stance, you will have turned through 360 degrees.

jumping kicks

Mention jumping kicks, and many people will visualise beautiful kicks forcing their way through the air to head height. Indeed, when jumping kicks are performed by a good martial artist, they are so good to watch that they invariably attract the attention of an audience. But unless a kickboxer has specialised in the technique and can execute it quickly, relatively few high, standard, jumping kicks are performed in the kickboxing ring.

Almost any kick that we have discussed so far can be performed as a jumping kick, giving you a lot of scope. But note that once you are in the air, it is difficult to change direction to perform another attacking or defensive kick. Remember that you are faster on the ground.

There are too many ways of preparing to perform jumping kicks for them all to be included here, so we will instead focus on the main jumping kicks: the jumping front kick and the jumping side kick.

the jumping front kick

There are different ways of preparing to perform a jumping front kick, depending on what you want the kick to achieve and how high you want to place it. It is important to remember that everybody has a different, and preferred, way of placing this kick.

The jumping front kick can be used as either an attacking or a defending technique. It can enable you to gain extra ground in order to move forwards and incorporate this technique into your attacking strategy or to get out of a situation that you are not controlling.

A traditional method of learning this kick appears opposite. Once you have mastered this technique, you can use the jumping front kick when you are moving backwards or forwards, and even when you are standing still.

The striking area is the ball or sole of the foot. Remember to pull back your toes and to ensure that your foot is pointing towards the target.

1 Assume a fighting stance, with your fists raised to protect your body and head.

2 Pull your non-kicking leg in a chambering position as high as you can towards your chest in order to gain height.

3 Then chamber your kicking leg just before it reaches the highest point.

4 Execute a front kick as though your foot were still on the ground. Pull your non-kicking leg towards your body and raise your fists to protect youself against any counterattack.

5 After you have perfomed the kick, snap back your leg and then land in a forward fighting stance.

the jumping side kick

The jumping side kick is probably the most famous of all of the jumping kicks, as well as the one that offers the most placement options. You can place the kick while running, stepping or standing still, or when moving backwards, forwards or again when stationary, in order to keep your opponent at a distance. The jumping side kick shown below is being performed from a fighting stance.

In a fight, you would probably not run into a jumping side kick because this would give your

1 Assume a fighting stance, with your fists raised to protect your body and head.

2 Gain height by pulling both your non-kicking and kicking leg into a chambering position as high as you can towards your chest.

3 Then turn your body and hip sideways in order to bring your kicking leg into a side-kicking position.

opponent a lot of notice that you intend to perform this kick. Running into a jumping side kick will, however, give you the most height.

The jumping side kick can be used as either an attacking or a defending technique or else simply to gain space in order to attack or retreat.

The striking area is the heel or the outside edge of the foot. Remember to pull back your toes and to flex your foot in order to avoid injury.

4 When you are jumping, as demonstrated above, it is important to pull your non-kicking foot towards your body.

5 Now execute a jumping side kick as though your feet were still on the ground. Ensure that you have pulled your non-kicking leg towards your body and have raised your fists to protect yourself against any counterattack.

6 After performing the kick, snap back your leg and land in a fighting stance.

low kicks and sweeps

There are two main low kicks: one directed at the outside of the thigh and the other, to the inside of the thigh. Both are similar to the roundhouse kick, except that the striking area is the shin.

Low kicks and sweeps are techniques that can be used to add variety to fighting styles and strategies. They are used in both kickboxing and Thai-boxing contests, although low kicks are not performed in full-contact fights in which all of the kicks are placed above the waist.

low kicks

Low kicks are effective techniques that can cause knockouts. Indeed, they can be so devastating that they make excellent self-defence applications.

1 An inside low kick being directed at the front of an opponent's inner thigh. The fighter doing the kicking uses his hip to whip his leg towards his opponent.

2 The outside low kick is similar to the inside low kick, except that the fighter doing the kicking aims for the outside of his opponent's thigh.

Note that these kicks are placed with the shin.

sweeping an opponent

The aim of the sweeping technique is to sweep your opponent off-balance, or even to throw him or her to the floor. When your opponent is off-balance, he or she will find it difficult to mount a defence against any further attack that you may be planning.

Before sweeping your opponent, remember that most of your weight should be on your sweeping leg.

To perform a sweep, aim the side of your foot at your opponent's foot, moving it inwards, towards the front of your opponent's leg.

The strikes discussed in this chapter can be performed with the knee or elbow. They are excellent close-quarter techniques that can be used very effectively in self-defence situations.

knee strikes

Knee strikes are simple, but effective, techniques that can have a devastating effect if executed correctly. Indeed, the knees are not commonly used in fights precisely because of the damage that they can cause. It is nevertheless important to grasp how knee strikes are performed because they are such effective applications when it comes to self-defence.

The knee strike can be aimed at the torso or the thigh, whose muscles may go into spasm and be afflicted by cramp when hit.

the front knee strike

The front knee strike is performed with your rear leg. Although the initial stages resemble those of a front kick (see page 130), at the point that you would place the front kick, you leave your knee in the chambering position and drive it forward, rather than upward, into the opponent's body or thigh. When you pull your opponent downwards, you will also have an opportunity to strike his or her head.

1 It is important to keep your guard up when your attacker comes forwards.

2 Chamber your rear leg and grasp your opponent as you bring your leg forwards.

3 When you execute the strike, make sure that you direct the force forwards, not upwards.

the outside knee strike

As its name suggests, the outside knee strike is executed from the outside of your body, the aim being to strike your opponent's floating ribs or thigh. The effectiveness of this technique is particularly evident if you watch Muay Thai matches, when you will see fighters getting their opponents in headlocks before executing the strike with either their rear or front legs.

1 Assume a fighting stance before executing an outside knee strike.

2 After grabbing your opponent's neck, lift your rear leg into a chambering position.

3 Pull your opponent towards you and then bring in your knee, aiming at the ribcage.

the jumping knee strike

The jumping knee strike is a technique that can be used to surprise an opponent. It is important that it is executed quickly. Grab your opponent's neck, jump up towards his or her body and strike either the head or ribcage.

1. Bring your rear leg forwards and grab your opponent's neck as you jump.

2. As you jump, thrust your knee forwards and strike your opponent's ribs.

caution

Knee strikes can be extremely powerful, so be very careful when practising them, especially when training with a partner.

elbow strikes

Elbow strikes are mainly used in Thai boxing and Muay Thai. Very powerful and dangerous techniques, the striking area is the elbow, which means that you are driving a pointed, hard bone towards your opponent. Elbow strikes are excellent attacking and defensive techniques that can be made at close range. When executing an elbow strike, remember that it is important to rotate your hips and shoulders in order to maximise the strike's power.

the front elbow strike

The front elbow strike follows a circular path towards the side of an opponent's head. The body movement is similar to that of a hook (see page 114), and it is important to turn your body into the strike.

1 If the distance between you and your opponent allows it, you can execute a front elbow strike in a fighting stance.

2 A close-quarter technique, the front elbow strike travels in a horizontal manner. Turn your whole body into the strike, pivoting on your front leg if necessary.

3 It is important to remember to allow your hips and rear leg to turn, too, in order to generate power. This strike can be placed with either the rear or lead hand.

the upward elbow strike

The upward elbow strike resembles an uppercut (see page 116), but instead of hitting your opponent with your fist, you use your elbow bone to strike his or her chin. This technique is an excellent way of getting past an opponent's defences.

1 Prepare to push past your opponent's defences by assuming a fighting stance.

2 The upward elbow strike can be performed with either your rear or lead hand, travelling vertically.

3 To gain extra power, use your leg to catapult you into making the upward elbow strike.

the downward elbow strike

The downward elbow strike, which is directed at the top of an opponent's head, can be used if he or she is below you. This technique can also be executed with a jump if you need to gain power and height. If you are to hit your target, it is crucial that you are close enough to your opponent to do so.

1 Before executing the downward elbow strike, make sure that your elbow is moving upwards slightly before striking downwards.

2 As you strike downwards, towards your opponent's head, make sure that you bring your body into the strike by bending your knees.

3 Turn your whole body into the strike as you raise your elbow to its highest point.

4 To gain extra power, use your body weight to help you to drop downwards.

the diagonal elbow strike

The diagonal elbow strike is probably the most effective elbow strike because it is directed above an opponent's guard before travelling diagonally across his or her face, starting at an eye and moving towards the nose. This technique is based on the same principle as that of the overhand right (see page 122).

This strike can be performed from both sides, with either the lead or rear arm. Note that it is always faster with the front arm, however, and therefore comes as more of a surprise to an opponent.

1 To gain power, simply raise your front foot (the foot that is on the same side as your striking elbow).

2 Before the executing the strike, move your elbow past your opponent's guard.

3 Stamp your foot at the same time as striking with your elbow.

the spinning back elbow strike

The spinning back elbow strike is normally used in conjunction with striking or kicking combinations. In order to execute the strike, you have to turn through 180 degrees. This means that your elbow is travelling further, thereby gaining power and momentum. Remember that you have to be quick if this strike is to succeed.

1 Turn your front foot so that your heel is pointing towards your opponent.

2 Turn your body through 180 degrees.

3 Now hit your opponent on the side of his or her head with your elbow.

12: **blocking**

When kickboxers cannot avoid blows being made against their bodies, they will try to block those blows in order to prevent any real damage from being inflicted on them.

blocking and avoiding punches

Avoiding blows being made to your head or body is part of your defence. Whatever you do that prevents an opponent from landing blows on your head or body is classified as a defensive move.

You can defend your body by parrying (redirecting a punch) or by blocking an attack, by slipping, by bobbing and weaving or by moving out of the way by side-stepping or by feinting.

Note that if it is to absorb the impact of a punch, a block has to be made as close to your body as possible

parrying

Parrying is a simple, but effective, way of redirecting a punch. It is normally used against a jab or right cross directed at your head. Parry with your lead hand, using only minimal movements, in order to redirect the force of the punch, which should miss your head by a small margin. The more you minimise your movements, the quicker you can return to the on-guard position.

Prepare to parry a jab in the fighting stance by unclenching your hand inside your boxing glove. When deflecting the jab with your hand, remember that minimising the move will enable you to counter your opponent's attack with a kick or a punch.

Prepare to parry a right cross in the fighting stance by first unclenching your hand inside your boxing glove. When deflecting the right cross with your hand, minimise the move in order to counterattack with a kick or a punch.

blocking

Blocking is a key skill that is very effective when you are not able to get away from a blow or are not fast enough to parry it. If you want to avoid receiving the blow, you will have to block it.

When you have practised these techniques often enough, you will automatically begin to know when to parry and when to block.

blocking punches to the body

Punches to the body are blocked with the elbow or forearm. While blocking, continue to move away, using minimal movements, from your opponent's fist in order to deflect the impact of the punch.

When blocking a jab to your body, turn your body and take the jab with your forearm or elbow.

When blocking a right cross, turn your body and take the right cross with your forearm or elbow.

This technique can be used to block any punch directed at the body, which is why it is important to practise different variations of this defensive block.

blocking punches to the head

Punches to the head are blocked with the elbow or forearm. While you are blocking a punch, continue to move away from your opponent's fist in order to deflect the impact of the punch.

When blocking a blow to the head, it is vital that you protect yourself by holding your elbows and arms tightly against your body. As your opponent's fist comes towards you, tuck your chin down, onto your chest, turn away your face slightly and try to let your glove take the impact of the punch.

blocking an uppercut

When blocking an uppercut directed at your chin, your technique should have elements of a parry and elements of a block. Which hand you use depends on the hand that your opponent is using to make the uppercut. Unclench your fingers inside your glove and block the punch as through you were parrying it, thereby stopping the uppercut's upward motion.

The uppercut shown above is being blocked by the defender's hand, which is open within the boxing glove, thus halting its upward motion. Don't reach for an uppercut lest you create a gap that your opponent can punch through.

When you use the double-arm block (left), it is crucial that you bring your elbows tightly together in order to take the impact of the punch.

slipping a punch

As the name of this technique suggests, when slipping a punch, you slip out of the punching area by moving your upper body and head, thereby not allowing your opponent to hit your head. This is obviously a very valuable skill to have in a fighting situation.

When slipping, bend at the waist and transfer your body weight to your front leg while turning your torso so that your shoulders and upper body are facing forwards.

When slipping out of a left jab's punching area, keep your guard up and bend your waist so that your weight is on your front leg, at the same time twisting your torso to avoid the punch.

To slip out of a right cross' punching area, perform the same movements as you would if you were evading a left jab, but turn to the other side.

the bob and weave

The bob and weave is used both to evade swinging punches aimed at your head and to create a moving target so that your opponent will find it difficult to aim for, and hit, your head. Move in a circular direction while shifting your head clear of the punch.

2 Your opponent's punch now whistles past your head.

1 While weaving, drop your body by bending your legs.

3 Move to the other side and come back up again with your guard in place. You are now in an excellent position to counterattack.

feinting

Feinting means moving your body backwards in order to remove yourself from your opponent's punching area, making it a very easy and effective way of evading a punch. In order to use feinting in a defensive manner, take a step back with your rear leg and try to leave your front leg positioned in front of your body.

1 When your opponent throws a punch, move your rear leg backwards.

2 Then move your body back, out of your opponent's reach.

Remember that you are moving your body partly to evade your opponent's punch and partly to make it more difficult for him or her to hit your head, a moving target always being harder to hit than a stationary one.

blocking and avoiding kicks

When you are defending your body against kicks, it is vital that you appreciate how powerful they can be. One thing that sets kickboxing apart from other competitive martial arts is that kicks can be directed towards an opponent's legs, which is why it is important to learn how to block them. Although you should learn how to avoid and block kicks, you will not always be able to fend off contact, which is why we will cover redirecting kicks on the following page.

blocking with the shin

Blocking with the shin is a very effective way of blocking a blow aimed at the thigh or calf. Imagine that you are the fighter pictured on the right in the photographs below, blocking the attack.

1 You are standing in a fighting stance when your opponent tries to direct a turning kick at your outer leg.

2 You shift your weight onto your back leg before raising your front leg and turning your body through 45 degrees so that your shin blocks your opponent's kick.

redirecting kicks

Redirecting a kick is a technique that is used to evade a front kick, a very powerful kick that is generally aimed at the middle of body. By redirecting the kick, you will effectively avoid receiving the full force of its impact, but will still be close enough to counterattack.

Use your left hand to redirect a front kick that your opponent is executing with his or her left leg. Make sure that you shift your body out of the way by moving your hips backwards and taking a small step to the opposite side of your opponent's kicking leg. This means that when your opponent kicks with his or her left leg, you take a small step to the right, and when the kick is made with the right leg, you take a small step to the left.

If your opponent kicks with his or her rear leg, step backwards before redirecting it.

1 A redirection is performed in the fighting stance. When redirecting a kick from your opponent's left leg, make sure that you move your body out of the path of the kick by taking a small step to the right. Also remember to pull your hips back.

2 Taking a step to the right ensures that you are safely out of the kick's path in case you don't catch your opponent's leg. Simultaneously block the kick and redirect it with the inner side of your boxing glove.

stepping into a kick and blocking it

Stepping into a kick can be seen as an offensive way of blocking it, the aim being to step into the path of the kick and to block its impact before counterattacking. This technique requires guts because rather than moving away from it, you will have to take the kick's impact, but there are times when you will have to steel yourself to do so, especially if you are dealing with a good kicker and need to break his or her kicking record. This technique is used against roundhouse kicks and spinning back kicks.

1 Perform the block in a fighting stance. Before stepping into the kick (in this case, a turning kick), make sure that your forearms are firmly positioned in protection of your body.

2 As your opponent's leg approaches your body, take a small step forward to give yourself more scope to launch a counterattack.

3 Now pivot on your front leg and turn your body into the kick, with both of your forearms continuing to protect your body.

the downward block

The downward block is normally used with a hip feint to ensure that you are not in the kick's path. It can be used to block a side or front kick that has taken you by surprise. The basic idea is that you pull back your hips to get out of the range of your opponent's kicking leg and simultaneously block the kick by swinging your front forearm downwards, using your elbow as a pivot. This move deflects the force of the kicking leg downwards. If you have under-estimated your opponent's kick, you can always jump backwards.

developing personal variations

All of the blocks and avoidance techniques discussed here are basic techniques, and kick-boxers develop their own variations of them. It is important that you develop your own style and variations that work for you. Most of your techniques should have one common feature, however, namely that you move with your opponents and use their force against them. Don't be rigid and static, because this would give an opponent an excellent target.

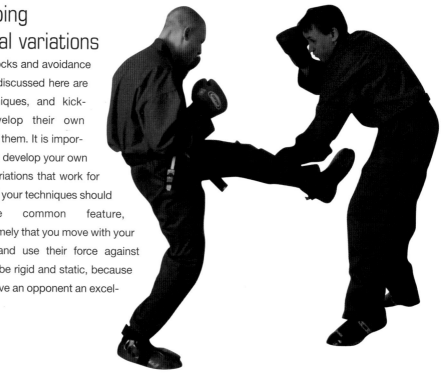

blocking and avoiding knee and elbow strikes

The effects of knee and elbow strikes can be devastating, which is why it is important to learn how to protect yourself against them. Doing so is easy, as long as you stay calm. But remember that it is vital that you practise these defences over and over again until they become second nature.

blocking elbow strikes

Defending yourself against an elbow strike is very similar to defending yourself against a hook. Your gloves should take the impact of a strike to your head. Even when you are blocking the strike, you should continue to move away from it in order to deflect its impact. When blocking a blow to the head, it is vital to hold your elbows and arms tightly against your body and head for protection. As the strike comes in, tuck your chin down, onto your chest, slightly turn your head away from the strike and try to take the impact with your gloves.

The same advice applies when blocking a blow to the other side. Always make sure that your elbows are firmly tucked against your body.

blocking knee strikes the 'X' block

The 'X' block is a simple block that is very useful for trapping an opponent's knee strike. As its name suggests, you cross your forearms in front of your body to create an 'X' shape, thereby taking the impact of the strike and preventing your opponent's knee from making contact with your body.

Your opponent is likely to combine a knee strike with a head-lock, which it is important for you to get out of (see the previous page for how to so do).

While in a fighting stance, and before the knee strike hits you, feint backwards with your hips and thrust both hands out and downwards. Cross your arms just above the wrists. Make sure that you block the strike on your opponent's thigh.

the one-arm block

Another simple way of blocking a knee strike is to use a one-arm block. This is particularly effective if your opponent has taken you by surprise. Holding your arm in front of your body, blocking the strike and taking its impact with your elbow will prevent your opponent's knee from making contact with your body.

While in a fighting stance, and before your opponent's knee hits you, feint backwards with your hips and block the strike with the arm that is closest to his or her knee. Make sure that you block the strike on your opponent's thigh.

pulling an opponent towards you

Pulling your opponent towards you is probably the simplest defence against a knee strike. When you have an inkling that he or she is likely to direct a knee strike at you, simply grab your opponent's waist and pull him or her towards you. This will ensure that your opponent lacks both the range and balance to execute a knee strike.

1 Move forwards as soon as you detect any hint of a knee strike. It may be that your opponent is trying to grab your neck, for instance.

2 Grip your opponent's waist and pull him or her towards you. When in the position shown above, your opponent will not be able to strike you with his or her knee.

sweeping an opponent

The sweep is a very effective technique to use against a knee strike. The idea is to parry the striking knee and sweep away your opponent's supporting leg. For example, when your opponent is performing a knee strike with his or her right leg, you slip your right arm under that leg and scoop it up, pushing your opponent off-balance with your other arm and sweeping away his or her supporting leg with your left leg. In this way, not only have you escaped from a headlock, you now have the upper hand because your opponent is lying on the floor.

1 When your opponent directs a knee strike at you with his or her right leg . . .

2 . . . parry it by moving to your left . . .

3 . . . and scooping up your opponent's leg with your right arm.

4 While you are still moving towards him or her, place your left hand on your opponent's shoulder, push him or her off-balance . . .

5 . . . and sweep away your opponent's supporting leg with your left leg.

getting out of a headlock

When you find yourself in a headlock, it is important to get out of this vulnerable position as soon as possible before your opponent decides to bombard you with a hail of devastating knee strikes. One way of doing this is to counter-attack with a headlock of your own.

1 The headlock is a strong hold. Try to create space between you and your opponent by pushing his or her head to the side. Do this by moving your left arm over your opponent's arms.

2 Your opponent's grip will slacken, creating a gap in his or her hold. Slide your right hand through the gap and grab your opponent's neck.

3 Now slip your left hand through the same gap.

4 You have now released your opponent's grip and can hold him or her in a headlock. You have the upper hand and can decide what to do next.

13: combinations in kickboxing

Having learned such different techniques as kicking, punching, moving, blocking and evading, it is crucial that your techniques flow. The more flowing they are, the faster you will execute them to your advantage, and the more fights you will win.

Because everyone's flexibility and body structure differ, and kickboxers all have different strengths and weaknesses, you will have to assess your physical make-up, skills and ability to perfect the combinations that work for you. It is important to find combinations that you can put to the most effective use.

Including a number of techniques in one movement, and being able to perform a variety of combinations, always sets a good kickboxer apart from an average one. Train with a view to using combinations in a variety of situations. Train to attack with combinations, to defend with combinations and to counterattack with combinations, all in a series of techniques that will throw your opponent's fighting style.

Remember that you should never use more than five techniques in a combination, for few fighters are able to deliver more than five powerful techniques in a combination.

By working on your combinations, you will improve the way that you perform techniques in different situations. You will also train your body to perform kicks and punches to a high standard, and will become more flexible and will improve your co-ordination, too. You will also gradually find that you are able to execute more complex techniques, as well as more advanced combinations.

In this chapter, we will look at some combinations, but note that there is actually an infinite number of combinations. If you study the combinations that follow, it will become clear that perfecting only a few techniques can give you an arsenal of combinations that you can modify to suit your personal ability.

The purpose of practising combinations in your training is to improve the way that your techniques flow, be it from side to side, backwards or forwards. It will also help you to mix your kicking and punching techniques in order to use them to their best effect in retreating or attacking situations. Learning to move, kick and punch in different positions will make you an unpredictable kickboxer. And if you are an unpredictable kickboxer, your opponent will find it harder to set you up to assume a position that is ideal for him, but not for you.

We will first look at punching combinations, then kicking combinations and finally, kicking and punching combinations. Both attacking and counterattacking techniques are demonstrated.

punching combinations

The first combination is a counterattack in which you are countering a jab.

1 The first thing that you have to do is avoid your opponent's jab. The quickest and simplest way of evading a left jab is to bob to the left, making sure that you move your face out of the striking area. Making this simple bob will enable you to remain within perfect striking range for a counterattack.

2 Having avoided the jab, counterattack with a left jab directed at your opponent's face.

3 Follow the jab with a right cross to your opponent's face. Note that you are utilising the jab's forward motion to generate more power for the right cross.

4 Due to the impact of your right cross, your opponent is probably moving backwards by this stage. If so, step towards your opponent and direct a hook at his or her midriff.

The second combination is an attack that you start with a left jab, followed by a right cross and then a left hook. If your opponent permits it, you could finish this combination with a right cross. When you perform these attacking techniques, remember to pull back your fist into a guarding position in case of a counterattack.

1 Look for an opportunity to land your left jab successfully.

2 Follow the jab with a right cross to your opponent's chin.

Ensure that you execute all of your punches in quick succession so that the sequence is fast.

3 The impact of your right cross will drive back your opponent's head. This gives you the perfect opportunity to aim a hook at the side of your opponent's head with your left fist.

4 In placing the hook, you are winding up your body to direct another right cross to your opponent's head.

The third combination is a counterattack that you can mount if your opponent is attacking your head with a left hook. Blocking the hook with your right arm and glove will turn your body away from the punch, placing you in a perfect position to direct a left hook at your opponent's body. You then land a right cross on your opponent's head and follow through with a jab.

1 Absorb the impact of your opponent's left hook with your right arm and glove as you turn your body away from your attacker.

2 Because you have turned your body and your opponent's midriff is exposed because he or she made the punch, you are now in a good position to counterattack with a left hook aimed at your opponent's body.

3 Next, raise yourself and throw a right cross at your opponent's jaw.

4 To finish the sequence, take a small step towards your opponent and then direct an jab at his or her chin.

In the fourth combination, you counter a right hook to your body by aiming an uppercut at your opponent's chin. You follow that with a left cross before finally directing a hook at the side of your opponent's head.

1 When your opponent directs a right hook at your body, block the punch and absorb the impact with your left arm, which should be held tightly against your body.

2 Now use your right arm to execute an uppercut. (This is a very effective way of using an uppercut to counterattack.)

3 Aim a left cross at your opponent's head.

4 Finally, use your right fist to deliver a hook to the side of your opponent's head.

The fifth combination is an attack that you start with a left jab, follow with another left jab and end with a right cross. After executing the first left jab, move forwards before throwing the second one. When performing these attacking techniques, remember to pull back your fist into a guarding position in order to be ready for a counterattack.

1 Before performing the first left jab, ensure that you have a realistic chance of landing it successfully.

2 Step towards your opponent before following the first left jab with a second to the chin, ensuring that you perform the sequence rapidly.

3 Now direct a right cross at your opponent's chin. The impact should push his or her head backwards, giving you an excellent opportunity to use another follow-on technique.

4 After delivering the right cross, pull your fist back into the guarding position as quickly as you can in order to be ready to defend yourself against a counterattack.

An attacking combination is being demonstrated on these pages. When you attack an experienced opponent, it's important to remember that single strikes will not be effective, which is why a combination must be used. This attack starts with a hook to the body, followed by an uppercut to the chin, then a hook to the side of the head and, finally, a powerful right cross to the head.

1 Keeping your guard up, lower yourself before directing a left hook at your opponent's side.

2 Now raise yourself and, using your right fist, aim an uppercut through the gap between your opponent's arms at his or her chin.

3 Turn your body into a left hook aimed at the side of your opponent's head.

4 Finish the combination by directing a right cross at your opponent's head.

kicking combinations

When performing kicking combinations, it's vital to understand that nearly every first kick leads the way for any follow-on kicks. This first kick can be used to distract, mislead or create space for the following kicks. The combination below is a very simple, but effective, way of distracting an opponent by faking a roundhouse kick to the midriff and then directing a roundhouse kick at the head.

1 Assume a fighting stance.

2 Using your rear leg, step towards your front, or kicking, leg so that the heel of your rear leg is pointing towards your opponent.

3 Now fake a low roundhouse kick. You will see your opponent lower his or her guard.

4 Pull back your leg.

5 Now aim a real roundhouse kick at your opponent's head.

Then pull back your leg as quickly as you can and either return to a fighting stance or execute further techniques.

The combination demonstrated on these pages is a very simple, but effective, way of distracting an opponent by sending a hook kick past his or her head and then delivering a surprise by coming back with a roundhouse kick, all in one movement.

1 Chamber your leg in preparation for executing a hook kick.

2 Distract your opponent by deliberately sending the kick past his or her head.

3 When your foot passes his or her head, pull it back and then aim a roundhouse kick at your opponent's head.

Pull back your foot as quickly as you can and either return to a fighting stance or perform further techniques.

The demonstration on these pages shows how you can effectively counterattack a front kick executed by your opponent by redirecting it. Doing this puts your opponent in a vulnerable position, which you can exploit by counterattacking with a kicking combination that starts with a front kick, followed by a spinning back kick.

1 As your opponent performs a front kick with his or her right, rear leg, redirect it with the palm of your left hand.

2 Now direct a fast and powerful front kick at your opponent's midriff.

3 Pull back your leg. Then turn your back on your opponent and position the foot that you have just pulled back so that its heel is pointing at your opponent. Turn your head and look over your left shoulder.

4 Perform a spinning back kick with your left leg. You can then either follow on with another technique or assume the fighting stance.

This kicking combination is an attack that firstly targets the midriff with a side kick and continues with a front kick to the midriff and then with a spinning hook kick to the head.

1 Standing in the fighting stance, whip your arms upwards. This motion will give your body upward momentum, shift all of your weight onto your front leg and cause your rear leg to move forwards.

2 Use this forward motion to execute a powerful side kick.

3 Now aim your rear leg at your opponent's midriff and perform a front kick. As you do so, ensure that your guard is in place to protect you from a counterattack.

4 Pull back your leg. Now turn your back on your opponent and position the foot that you have just pulled back so that its heel is pointing at your opponent. Turn your head and look over your left shoulder. Execute a spinning hook kick with your left leg.

Either follow on with further techniques or resume the fighting stance.

The combination demonstrated here is used to create space for a kick when your opponent is too close to enable you to execute one effectively. Simply push him or her away with a front kick and follow that up with a roundhouse kick.

1 When you and your opponent are standing very close to one another, the normal response would be to use your fist. Your opponent is probably expecting that, however, so surprise him or her.

2 Starting in a fighting stance, execute a front kick with your rear leg. As you kick, thrust your hips forward and drive the ball of your foot through your opponent's guard.

3 Your front kick has forced your opponent backwards. Now move your kicking leg to the fore.

4 Having created sufficient space with your front kick, you are now in a perfect position to perform a roundhouse kick.

Use this combination to stop your opponent from coming towards you by executing a powerful side kick and then following it with a jumping front kick directed at his or her body.

1 Your opponent approaches as you are standing with your kicking leg to the fore. Chamber your front leg and hop backwards slightly in order to gain space for a side kick. Now keep your opponent at bay by aiming a side kick at him or her.

2 Then launch yourself off your supporting leg into a jumping front kick directed at your opponent's body and push him or her away.

Having regained your space, you are now in a position to perform any technique you like.

This attack sequence is very fast and effective. The idea is to fake a front kick to your opponent's midriff, chamber your leg and direct a roundhouse kick at his or her head. Next, you position your kicking leg in front of you so that your heel is pointing at your opponent before turning your body and aiming a back kick at your opponent's midriff with your other leg.

1 Assume a fighting stance, chamber your leg and fake a front kick.

2 Chamber your leg and turn your supporting foot so that its heel is pointing at your opponent, turning your body at the same time. Now direct a roundhouse kick at your opponent's head.

3 Do not chamber your kicking leg, but instead turn your body and position your kicking foot next to your supporting foot. Look over your shoulder, chamber the leg on the same side and unleash a back kick at your opponent's midriff.

Use this combination when you have to use footwork to overcome the distance between you and your opponent. Aim a roundhouse kick at his or her head, chamber your kicking leg and then direct a front kick at your opponent's midriff.

1 Standing in a fighting stance, whip your arms upwards to shift all of your weight to your front leg and cause your rear leg to move forwards. Using this forward momentum, execute a roundhouse kick.

2 Chamber your kicking leg and then position it in front of you. Now perform a front kick and push your opponent away with the sole of your foot.

kicking and punching combinations

Having looked at kicking and punching combinations separately, we will now explore how to score points by combining kicks and punches. You can use hand techniques to set you up for performing kicks, and kicks to set you up for executing punches.

We will start with a simple, but effective, combination that includes a front kick followed by a jab and then a right cross to the head. It does not matter how you start the combination, but in this example, a front kick is used to create an opening in the opponent's defence.

1 Stand in a fighting stance and chamber your back leg. Now direct a front kick at your opponent's midriff. Your opponent will concentrate on defending his or her midriff, creating an opening at head height.

2 After performing the front kick, position your kicking leg in front of your body and aim a jab at your opponent's head, all in one movement.

3 Now throw a right cross. It's important to ensure that this punch to the head quickly follows the other.

The second combination starts with a punching sequence consisting of a left jab followed by a powerful right cross and then a left hook to the head. The combination ends with you pushing your opponent away with a front kick in order to prevent him or her from launching a punching counterattack.

1 Execute a left jab in the fighting stance.

2 Bring back your left fist to guard your face and then direct a right cross at your opponent's head.

3 Bring back your right fist in order to protect your face and then aim a left hook at your opponent's head.

4 Now perform a front kick with your front leg, pushing your opponent away with the sole of your foot.

This combination serves to counterattack a roundhouse kick, enabling you to execute a roundhouse kick of your own and then to follow it up with a right cross, an uppercut and another right cross to the head. The sequence ends with a side kick directed at your opponent's midriff.

1 Block your opponent's roundhouse kick.

2 Push your opponent's leg down and across in front of you. This puts you in an excellent position to counterattack with a kick.

3 Now direct a roundhouse kick at your opponent's head.

4 Move your kicking leg in front of you and use the forward momentum to aim a right cross at your opponent's head.

6 Quickly follow the uppercut with another right cross.

5 Pull back your right fist to protect your head and then perform an uppercut with your left fist.

7 Now lean back and chamber your front leg. If you are too close to your opponent to do this, hop backwards on your supporting leg in order to gain distance.

8 Perform a side kick to keep your opponent at a safe distance.

This combination uses an axe kick to create an opening in an opponent's head-area defence in order to place a hook. This is quickly followed by an uppercut, then by a jab, and finally by a front kick.

1 Use your front leg to direct an axe kick at your opponent's defence.

2 Now that your opponent's guard is down, follow through with a right hook.

3 Having pulled back your right fist in order to protect yourself against an attack, execute an uppercut with your left fist.

4 Throw a jab with your left fist and direct a front kick at your opponent's midriff in order to keep him or her away from you.

varying and adapting combinations

Once you have mastered the necessary punching and kicking skills, there is no limit to the number of variations that can be made to the combinations outlined in this book.

Always adapt combinations to suit your skill level, personal fighting style and physical strengths and weaknesses. Select those techniques that you are good at to integrate into your way of fighting by creating combinations that suit you.

14: using kickboxing as a form of self-defence

There is a perception that kickboxing is more of a contact sport than a martial art that can be used effectively in a self-defence situation. This could not be further from the truth, however.

Imagine a situation in which you are fighting in a competition and are being attacked by an opponent. Your first thoughts will no doubt be, 'How can I minimise the impact of the attack?' 'How can I defend myself against this attack?' And 'How can I counterattack?' This is exactly what you would think in a self-defence situation, but if you made a mistake, you would be more likely to end up being hurt.

When you are training in kickboxing, you are therefore training your mind and body to cope with any self-defence situation. Thus you will start to work on your self-defence techniques the day that you take up kickboxing.

If a kickboxer can throw powerful kicks and punches in the ring, he or she can certainly do the same on the streets in order to fight off a thug when all peaceful means have failed.

Indeed, the techniques used in kickboxing are very effective in a self-defence situation. People who practise more traditional martial arts can sometimes be lulled into an unrealistic frame of mind because little or no contact is used. How can you learn what kind of power a punch or kick can pack if you have never been on the receiving end of these techniques? In kickboxing, by contrast, you will learn how the impact of a punch feels and will know how much power a kick or punch can generate. Receiving a hard, well-placed kick or punch will not come as a shock to a kickboxer, and these techniques are best first experienced in a training situation than on the streets. Indeed, the shock of sustaining a powerful kick or punch can be a very important learning curve. You will learn to overcome that

shock and will develop the will to carry on and defend yourself. You will learn to prepare yourself mentally to be hurt, and will overcome your fear in order to defend yourself.

The main difference between being attacked in the ring and on the streets is that your attacker will not be wearing gloves on the streets, and because he or she wants to hurt you, you will not be attacked in a sporting manner either. You may also be attacked by more than one person. This is when the rules of combat change and you may have to attack first in order to get away unharmed. Your instincts will tell you when to strike or whether the situation can be resolved in a civil manner.

Because it teaches you superb self-defence techniques, more and more women are taking up kickboxing. You will be trained to

deal with realistic situations, and will consequently learn what is possible and what is not when defending yourself. Kickboxing simultaneously shows you your limits and capabilities.

In short, all kickboxing techniques can have self-defence applications. Self-defence kickboxing also uses techniques that are disallowed in the ring. These include striking at such areas as the eyes, groin, knees and Adam's apple, to name but a few.

self-defence techniques

The following techniques are designed to familiarise you with some simple, but effective, self-defence sequences. Should you find yourself in a combat situation, emotions will be running high, and when you are feeling deeply stressed, easy sequences are often the most effective way of getting you out of a difficult situation.

1 There is still some distance between you and the attacker, but he is moving closer.

2 Raise your hands so that your palms are facing the attacker. This can be perceived as a goodwill gesture ('Let's talk'). But if the aggressor decides to attack, you have raised your arms and are ready to defend yourself.

3 The attacker is too close to enable you to land an effective punch. An elbow strike is perfect for a situation like this. The main targets are the temples, cheekbones, nose and jaw. Remember to turn your body into the elbow strike.

4 Because you are still very close to the attacker, now's the time to use another close-range technique. Direct your knee at his groin, grab his neck and then, with a powerful hip action, drive your knee forwards, into his groin.

In this scenario, the aggressor makes it clear that he will attack you. This means that you will have to attack him first in order to prevent him from injuring you. Low kicks are quick and excellent ways of stopping an attacker. They are directed at the groin and knee here, followed by a jab-and-uppercut combination.

1 The aggressor prepares to attack you.

2 Prepare your guard and kick the attacker in the groin area with your front leg.

3 Follow up the first kick by aiming a low roundhouse kick at the attacker's knee with the shin of your other leg.

4 Now direct a right jab at the attacker's head.

5 Finish the situation by throwing a left upper-cut at the attacker's jaw.

3

The combination demonstrated here deals with an attack from behind. When the attacker grabs your right shoulder to intimidate you, react by reaching behind his arm and simulating an uppercut. Follow this with a palm strike before pushing him away.

1 The attacker suddenly grabs your right shoulder from behind.

2 Raise your right arm and turn sideways, towards the attacker.

3 As you turn, try to bring your foot behind the attacker's heel and reach behind his arm, bringing your fist and forearm in front of his arm as if you were about to throw an uppercut. This move will both damage the attacker's shoulder and enable you to grasp him firmly.

4 Now direct a palm strike at the attacker's nose. Then release your hold and push the attacker away from you.

If you find yourself being strangled by an attacker, use simple, but powerful, techniques to escape his hold. Quickly move your right arm in a circle before finishing with a kick to the groin and a left cross to the head.

1 The attacker is strangling you.

2 Extend your right arm to almost its full extent and move it in a clockwise circle.

3 With your arm over the attacker's arm, twist your upper body anticlockwise as you step back with your left foot. You will find that he releases his hold.

4 Now aim a kick at the attacker's groin.

5 Follow up with a left cross.

5

If you are grabbed from behind so that both of your arms are immobilised, your first move should be to head-butt the attacker's nose or face. Then stamp your heel on the attacker's foot and grab a finger or thumb (whichever is the easiest to get hold of) and twist it away from your body to release the hold. After that, direct a backward elbow strike at the attacker's floating rib and a side kick at his knee.

1 The attacker has grabbed you from behind.

2 First head-butt the attacker.

3 Then stamp on the attacker's foot with your heel.

4 Now grab a finger or thumb to force the attacker to release his hold.

5 Next, direct a backward elbow strike at the attacker's floating ribs.

6 Finally, aim a side kick at the attacker's knee.

When you are dealing with two attackers, you will have to react fast. If the first attacker tries to reach for you or punch you, counterattack by directing a kick at his or her groin. Then turn around and aim a low side kick at the second attacker's knee before quickly leaving the scene.

1 It is clear that one of the attackers is about to strike you or lunge at you.

2 To defend yourself, direct a front kick at the first attacker's groin.

3 Swiftly turn and aim a side kick at the second attacker's knee with your other leg. Now leave the scene by walking backwards so that you keep both attackers in your sights.

This self-defence application enables you to escape from a neck hold when an attacker has positioned his or her arms around your arms and neck. This is a very dangerous position to find yourself in because the attacker could easily break your neck. You will therefore have to move quickly.

1 Should you find yourself in a neck hold . . .

2 . . . raise your arms and body as high as you can . . .

3 . . . and then forcefully come back down again, pushing your arms downwards and lowering your body all in one move. As you come down, stamp on your attacker's foot.

4 Once the attacker has released his or her hold, take a step away and aim a back elbow strike at his or her nose.

You now find yourself in a very difficult situation. You are lying on the ground and an attacker is coming at you. Try to get up as quickly as possible, but if you can't, ensure that the front of your body is always facing the attacker because this will put you in the best position to defend yourself with your arms and legs. If you then have the opportunity to kick your attacker's knee, do so before aiming a kick at his or her groin.

1 You are lying on the ground and the attacker is about to kick you. Defend yourself by cocking your leg in front of your body at an angle of 90 degrees so that it takes the blow.

2 Should the attacker move round to your other side, turn your body as he moves in order to protect your back. Now position the foot that is closest to the ground behind the attacker's heel and direct a side kick at his or her knee.

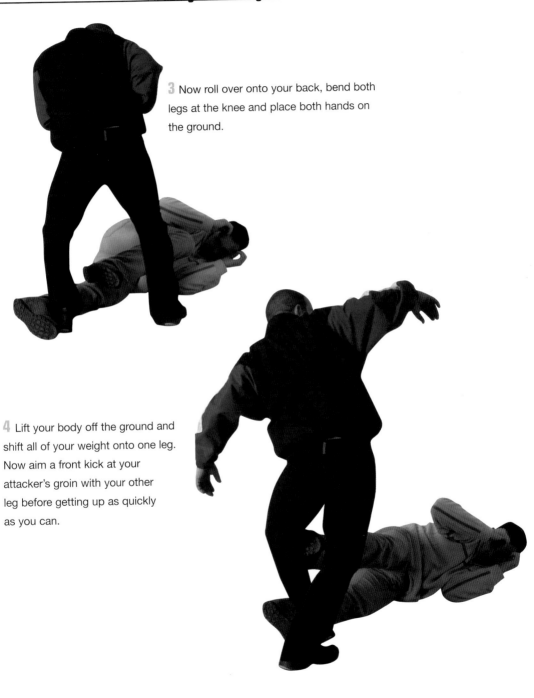

3 Now roll over onto your back, bend both legs at the knee and place both hands on the ground.

4 Lift your body off the ground and shift all of your weight onto one leg. Now aim a front kick at your attacker's groin with your other leg before getting up as quickly as you can.

9

The next attack is very nasty. You cannot see the attacker who is choking you and have to react quickly. Simply grab his or her arm, drop down onto one knee and throw him or her over your shoulder. Once the attacker is on the ground, you could aim a kick at the side of his or her body.

1 Your attacker is choking you from behind.

2 Pull on the attacker's arm and go down on one knee, positioning your foot on the outer side of your attacker's foot.

3 It is important that you sink onto the knee that is on the same side as the elbow of the arm that is choking you. Now make yourself as small as possible and throw the attacker over your shoulder.

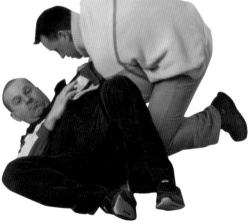

4 Get up and grasp the attacker's arm.

You may have to defend yourself against an attacker who has a weapon, in this case a knife. If so, take the attacker by surprise by firmly grabbing the hand holding the knife with both hands and diving under his or her arm. (If you straighten the attacker's arm when you come back up again, you will break it.) Now direct a back fist at the attacker's nose.

1 The attacker is threatening you with a knife.

2 Grab the attacker's hand.

3 Now position the attacker's hand on your shoulder and pull it down as you rise up. (If this move is performed forcefully, you will break the attacker's arm.)

4 Pulling down the attacker's arm will force him or her to drop the weapon.

5 Now direct a back fist at the attacker's nose.

index

credits and acknowledgements

I would like to thank my partner, Amy, for her love, patience and support during the writing of this book. I would also like to thank Ray Pawlett for his advice, invaluable support and friendship.

Last, but not least, my thanks to Dave, Leanne and Mark, very skilful kickboxers whose help during the photo-shoot was greatly appreciated.

DAVE GENTRY Third-degree black belt in kickboxing. Trainer of the current men's, women's and junior PKA British champions. First place three-man team-event-winner 2001 and 2002. Third place three-man team-event-winner 2003, PKA British championships. PKA instructor of the year 2003. Full-time professional area instructor, London region. www.kickboxing-london.co.uk

LEANNE PHILLIPS Brown belt in kickboxing. Junior PKA British champion 2002 and 2003. Third place three-man team-event-winner 2003.

MARK BLUNDELL Brown belt in kickboxing. Full-time, qualified, kickboxing coach.